Mayur T. Dalal

Dear Tom.
    Nice meeting you
last month at pacific
office. Enjoy the book
& send me your feed back.
& Lets stay in touch
                    8/1/15

Achieve Emotional Freedom | A

Achieve Emotional Freedom

And Grow
your Relationships
exponentially

Creating Certainty
& Predictibility
for generations to come

Author : Mayur T. Dalal

      30 Hunt Court Jericho NY11753
      917-359-4818
      Mdalal8688@gmail.com

Publisher name : Sister Nivedita Publication
      3, Balmukund Plots, Rajkot
      Gujarat, India

Cover Design
and Book Design : Dotad

Printed by : Girish Offset

ISBN : 978-93-81314-21-0

First printing 2017

References

The Positive Focus®, Unique Ability®, Unique Process™, and The GAP™ are all trademarks created and owned by The Strategic Coach Inc.

Know your score ©2016 The Strategic Coach Inc .

All rights reserved. Used with written permission.

Planning Horizon Graphic courtesy Legacy Companies Used with permission.

Achieve Emotional Freedom   D

The information contained in this book is intended to provide helpful and informative material on the subject addressed. It is not intended to serve as a replacement for professional advice. Any use of the information in this book is at the reader's discretion. Although the author and publisher have made every effort to ensure that the information in this book was correct at press time, the author and publisher do not assume and any liability to any party for any loss, damage, or disruption caused by errors or omissions, whether such errors or omissions result from negligence, accident,

Client names, circumstances and other personal information included in this book have been changed to protect privacy.

INTRODUCTION 1

PART 1 : THE PROCESS..7

    CHAPTER 1 : THE PROCESS AND ME—HUMBLE BEGINNINGS 8

    CHAPTER 2 : PLOTTING THE COURSE FOR

    A MULTI-GENERATIONAL ROADMAP 28

PART 2 : THE MEHTA'S..39

    CHAPTER 3 : MEET THE MEHTA'S 40

    CHAPTER 4 : THIRTEEN TOXIC ENERGIES 49

    CHAPTER 5 : THE ANTIDOTE TO TOXICITY 55

    CHAPTER 6 : STUMBLING BLOCKS AND PROGRESS 60

    CHAPTER 7 : MEHTA FAMILY UPDATE 63

PART 3 : THE SMITH'S 67

    CHAPTER 8 : MEET THE SMITH'S 68

    CHAPTER 9 : OPENING HEARTS AND EXPANDING MINDS 82

    CHAPTER 10 : SMITH FAMILY UPDATE 94

PART 4 : THE CORDERO'S 97

    CHAPTER 11 : MEET THE CORDERO'S 98

    CHAPTER 12 : REALIGNING FOCUS 105

    CHAPTER 13 : CORDERO FAMILY UPDATE 113

PART 5 : AN INVITATION 116

    CHAPTER 14 : ARE YOU READY TO SHARE AND GROW? 117

    CHAPTER 15 : Values-based Family Governance 124

    ABOUT THE AUTHOR 130

    ACKNOWLEDGEMENTS 132

Dedicate

For Grandfather and Father,
whose humble grace and
quiet wisdom
continue to guide me
in all I do.

In the joy of others,
lies our own
In the progress of others,
rests our own
In the good of others,
abides our own

Know this to be the key to peace
And happiness

- HDH Pramukhswami Maharaj
BAPS

Introduction

*What binds us together generation
after generation is not necessarily
the answers we uncover,
but the virtues discovered in the search.*

There are far too many broken hearts among people who hold significant financial wealth today. I am witness to these broken hearts every day in my work as a wealth coach for high net worth families. The elders of these families have been enormously successful in the enterprises they've created, yet they fear that they don't have what it takes to transform and sustain their vision and wisdom into the future. They've given unconditionally of their time, talent and treasure, yet their generosity has often led to deep dysfunction and feelings of entitlement among their younger generations. Few people in these families think of themselves as part of a loving, cooperative circle that endeavors to make a better world. Instead, it's every man for himself. The overarching question on their lips is, "What's in it for me?" rather than "How can we come together to make a difference for the common good?"

This lack of cooperation leads to a lot of resentment. It leads to confrontation, discomfort, disillusionment, disappointment, anxiety, and worst of all, a lack of empathy. At the center of all this turmoil stands the family leader who desperately wants to make things right but lacks the clarity to do so. They simply have no idea where to start.

As the patriarch or matriarch of a family with high net worth, does any of this sound familiar to you? Can you relate?

If so, then this book is for you. The process I will describe here—the Legacy Perpetuator™ process—leads to a wealth transfer plan that does more than just help

you take control of your resources. It is a process that helps you create a family legacy and develop a total strategy for multi-generational life harmony. It builds a better understanding of who you are as a family right now and provides a custom roadmap for where you want to go together in the future. In essence, it results in a multi-generational succession plan.

We carefully craft and meticulously implement your family's exclusive Life Harmony Plan for the next 25, 50, 75 and 100 years. Taking this long-term perspective leads to outstanding benefits, such as:

- A continuous sense of purpose

- Peace and tranquility within yourself and in relation to others

- A profound positive impact on every relationship

- Lasting financial prosperity

By using our specialized knowledge solutions to examine and fine-tune all aspects of your financial life as well as your current and future goals, we can help you achieve a perspective that's more balanced and holistic than you can get any other way. We'll work with you to develop customized solutions for maximizing

Handing Down Values for the Ages

If your experience growing up was anything like mine, you learned your values by observing how your parents and grandparents did what they did and listening to what they shared with you. Our patriarchs and matriarchs created their own futures and were effective in transferring to us their values, their wisdom and their understanding of family governance, and we followed their leads. But what we're seeing today are major gaps between family leaders and the generations that follow them; gaps in the form of communication, expectation management and mindset. What the Legacy Perpetuator™ process is all about is creating a plan for consciously, deliberately, effectively passing on your wealth, values and wisdom in such a way that it brings your family members together rather than driving them apart. And once you and your family have this plan in place, your outcomes and outlook will never be the same again.

Remember, nobody else can dictate the extent to which you can empower yourself in the future.

First you must identify and break yourself free from toxic thoughts and beliefs. You cannot create a new and better world by relying on old world thinking.

You can create a better world by shifting your mindset. But this is not a do-it-yourself endeavor.

You must align yourself with someone who you can serve as an enlightened partner for you, someone who can become a mentor and a guide in the process, let the Legacy Perpetuator™ process be our framework. It would be my profound blessing and honor to lead you through it.

We will begin our partnership with this book, in which we will explore the Legacy Perpetuator™ process as it was applied to three fictional families: one led by a highly successful corporate executive; another led by the creator of a $100 million company; and a third led by husband and wife health professionals who were tops in their respective fields. In the chapters ahead, you will learn about:

- How the elements of Discovery, Evaluation, Implementation, and Sustainability lead to the creation of a multi-generational Emotional Freedom via the Legacy Perpetuator™ process

7 Step Legacy Perpetuator Process™

Unique Journey

Vision Mission Purpose for next 50 years

Perpetual Gift of Wisdom and Wealth To 3 Generation

Quartely and Annual Progress Report to create sustainability

Discovery and Gap Analysis

Evaluate Choices and Implement customized Strategies

Establish 12 Urgent and Importannt goals for next 3 years

- Concrete steps to enable each family member to grow stronger *emotionally, spiritually, physically, and in relation to one another*

- How to create more empathy, empowerment, inspiration, and clarity in the family unit
- A means for measuring and tracking your level of family harmony.
- A matrix that can increase family unity by illustrating the values important to each family member, and exposing which values are shared by whom
- And much more!

Building wealth may have been your overarching mission as a family leader, and you've done well in that regard. But even more important to your family's well-being is the harmony you will create through the virtues of enhanced clarity, conviction and vision. Once you've established these three treasured virtues within yourself, you can then preserve them and pass them along with your wealth to your family for generations to come. This will be your legacy... your heritage of harmony and abundance. Someday your descendants will look back with profound gratitude upon all you've done, and they will salute you for undertaking this process. They will acknowledge that because of your love, determination and foresight, your family truly does have it all.

And so with
open hearts
and minds,
let us explore
the process
now.

PART 1:
THE PROCESS

Building Foundation
for Emotional Freedom

Chapter 1:

The Process and Me—Humble Beginnings

From the lessons offered through the tapestry of time,
I sift courage, love, integrity, wisdom, and passion.

For the last 56 years of my life, my day has started precisely at 4:30 a.m. I have my dear paternal grandfather, Harkisondas Dalal, to thank for that. Grandpa began waking me at that early hour every morning when I was three-years old. He would rouse me gently, make me smile, get me ready, and then out the door we would march hand-in-hand, walking together two kilometers down the dusky streets of Bombay to go to Temple. Along the way he would tell me stories of his life, his father's life, my father's life. On the way back home he would tell me even more stories and share even more wisdom with me. His words still echo in my heart to this day:

"To care for others, Mayur, you must start by becoming self-conscious. Not selfish or insecure, but self-conscious. Always take care of yourself first so you will have enough energy to share with your family, your friends, your neighbors, the strangers you will meet…"

"Move through the world with gentleness, Mayur. Do selfless acts of kindness every single day. Give all that you have, then dig deeper and give some more…"

"There will come moments in your life when you will be confused and not know how to proceed. In those moments, be still; be patient and practice gratitude. Trust that your right path will be revealed, and it will. It will…"

How I wish every child could have experiences such as I had with my grandfather on those walks. What a treasure he gave to me!

During those years of walking to Temple with my grandfather, An awareness was created within me; an intention. I became laser focused on executing the divine blessings of my grandfather and applying his wisdom in every aspect of my life. I became self-conscious in a healthy way, deliberately focusing on my personal growth and well-being so I could give my best to others. I was not mature enough at seven years of age to understand all that my future might hold, but I had unwavering faith that my grandpa could not be wrong about me.

That experience of waking before dawn and walking to Temple with Grandpa became part of my DNA. He has been gone from this earth since 1966, but even now—as I approach my 60th birthday—I still rise every morning precisely at 4:30 a.m. without any alarm or wakeup call.

My grandfather's wisdom of "Unless you do one selfless act of kindness every day, you do not have permission to go to bed!" was my first golden nugget in life.

The second golden nugget came from my father, Thakorbhai Dalal. Dad lost his beloved mother when he was only three-years old. My grandfather never remarried. My father and his two siblings were raised by Grandfather's younger brother's wife, who already had five children of her own. Thanks to her generosity, my grandfather was freed from worry about his kids and was able to devote time to running his business. By the time my dad was eight-years old, he understood the sacrifice his aunt was making to care for eight children. He decided to show his respect by contributing to the household. He began tutoring classmates earning one rupee for each session. That was a lot of money for a young boy in India in the 1930s.

But my father had his sights set on bigger things than tutoring for few rupees. When he was 16-years old he joined the university. Shortly after he arrived on campus, the contractor running the cafeteria inside the dormitory quit with short notice. Father went to the dean of the school and said, "Would it be okay if I take over operation of the cafeteria? I promise I can do a good job without sacrificing my grades." The dean agreed to let him try, and my father set about the task. In doing so he created a profitable business and an empowering work environment in which students from families with low incomes could earn money to apply toward their tuition, and even have some spending cash left over. It was a winning situation for the university, the student workers and my father. As a result, Dad made his first million rupees before he turned 21. He went on to create a thriving business of his own. Things were good for our family… or so we thought.

But alas, my dear grandfather became ill in 1966 after the passing of his younger brother. He knew he was not going to live much longer, so before he became incapacitated he disclosed to the family that he would be leaving behind considerable debt. India was just coming out of a war with Pakistan which had had a devastating effect on many businesses, including my grandfather's. When my dad and his brother learned of Grandfather's debt, they met to decide what to do about it. My father—the youngest brother—expected that he and his sibling would tackle the problem together, but at the end of the day my dad was the only one willing to take it on. The elder brother was worried. He feared that assuming responsibility for the debt would destroy his family's financial security.

"I understand your position," my father told his brother. "Everything will be okay. I will see to it."

Dad went back to my grandfather and told him not to worry, that the family would take care of the debt. Shortly thereafter my beloved grandfather passed away. I was eight-years old at the time. For the next eight years, I watched my parents struggle. My father literally had to let go of his own successful business in order to honor the commitment he'd made to his father. He fought for years to pay off Grandfather's debt. Mother sold all of her jewelry to support us. Three assets we had as a family were compassion, care and hope. I was the eldest child, and like my father before me, I started tutoring to bring in some financial resources to support my younger siblings.

And also like my father before me, I graduated from high school at age 16 with top honors.

I was given a national scholarship by the President of India for my undergraduate studies, but even with a scholarship, going away to university would take money… money we did not have. Therefore I attended university close to home, walking four km a day so I didn't have to spend bus fare. I completed my undergraduate program in 1978 and continued on to graduate school. I graduated with a degree in chemical engineering in 1981 and was accepted in a U.S. university's Ph.D. program. But my father intervened. He told me that he would like for me to earn an MBA instead. He encouraged me to be an outlier and become an entrepreneur. And then he said this to me, which is the second golden nugget in my life:

Right now everyone knows you as my son, Mayur. But **if you can create an outcome where everyone knows me as your father, then I will be happy.** Only then I will be fulfilled. Your achievements and all your contributions to society must be such that everybody knows me as your father.

Now, that's a tall order for a 21-year old! But I accepted my father's challenge because I wanted to please him, and because I trusted him completely. If he thought I had what it took to be a great entrepreneur, then I knew I must try. I also wanted to live up to his example. He had done a truly remarkable thing by earning one million rupees by age 21. And at age 35 at the peak of his professional career, he gave up everything to honor the commitment he'd made to his father without knowing if he would be able to support his family. To match his level of sacrifice, courage and nobility, I knew I would have to work ten times harder.

I applied to four prestigious business schools—the Ivy League of India—and I was accepted by all of them. But out of necessity we made the decision for me to stay in Bombay so we would not have to pay for room and board. Within five years' time I had earned my MBA and was teaching the curriculum to students. I served as a board member of the Rotary Club and the Masonic Lodge. And two years later, at age 28, I became the youngest business head for a multinational in India.

My job with this multinational company soon brought me to the United States. By then I was married to my lovely wife, Madhavi, and we had been blessed with our son Sagar, and daughter, Reema. I recall my father-in-law telling me that if I could succeed in India at such a young age, I could do miracles in America, the land of opportunity. Sky was the limit, he said. He encouraged me to explore other career options outside the multinational company I was working for. I thought to myself, why would somebody like me, at the top of his game in leadership, *in mentoring, in financial wherewithal give up all of that and start something new and unknown?*

But the more I thought about it, the more attractive the idea of change became. After all, my grandfather and father had always encouraged me to reach higher… to think outside the box… to not fear adversity… to trust my intuition… to trust God.

So I applied to a blind ad in the New York Times and I was quickly hired by a financial services firm, leading me to quit my job as business head of the multinational company. My excitement over my new occupation was soon replaced with regret. I had no idea what the hell I was doing in this new career of mine. I was a complete novice. I had no experience with the financial market, no knowledge of tax strategies. My familiarity was with the Indian financial system, not the American one. It was an extremely difficult time for me. I began beating myself up and second guessing my decision. I was struggling.

Although I tried to hide my worries from my wife, she saw how stressed I was. One evening after dinner in our little studio apartment, she came to me and said, "I know you very well, Mayur. I see you. I observe you. You are not happy. I don't think you enjoy what you're doing here. You are lost. Your energy and vitality for living are gone. I have seen you succeed in everything you have done. I don't think you are passionate about what you're doing."

At that point I asked Madhavi to please leave me alone so I could think, which was funny because we were in a studio apartment... where was she supposed to go? She smiled, nodded and sat in one corner while I sat in another corner across the room. As I sat there with tears stinging my eyes, my grandfather's words came back to me:

"There will come moments in your life when you will be confused and not know how to proceed. In those moments, be still; be patient and practice gratitude. Trust that your right path will be revealed, and it will. It will..."

And so I sat silently, patiently, prayerfully, gratefully in my corner for a period of quiet introspection. By the time I was finished an hour later, I had a blueprint for the way forward. My resolve was renewed and my self-confidence was restored. I was carrying the responsibility of providing for a newborn, a two-year old, and my wife, who believed in me wholeheartedly. I would not let them down, nor would I dishonor the memory of my wise grandfather by giving up. Neither would I disappoint my father. I would not allow him to become known as the father of a loser.

I decided to shift my focus from being helpless in a new country to exploring opportunities to build my own practice. I told my wife that I would not be keeping my current job, nor would I be returning to the multinational company, which had offered to hold my position for a time just in case I changed my mind. I would carve out a career path that made the most of my abilities; a career path in which I could use my God-given gifts and talents to make the world a better place. My grandfather's wisdom of giving all you have and then giving even more would become the foundation for my work going forward.

I made the decision to put my primary focus on working with physicians to improve their financial wellbeing. I conducted a focus group, and the result of that meeting was my commitment to create a new business opportunity. For the next three years, from 1988 to 1991, I worked 100 hours a week and became a national resource to medical doctors for asset protection, retirement planning and insurance, representing Equitable Life. In 1992 I was promoted to sales manager and asked to be a team builder. From 1992 to 1996 we built a team of bankers, CPAs and other committed professionals, and I became a top ten developing leader. During this time of great success and hard work, I also kept my community impact commitment, serving as president of Lad Vanik Samaj of North America, vice president for the Association of Indians in America, and vice president of Gujarati Samaj of New York. I was then offered a position as a branch manager in California.

Around that time my father was diagnosed with a tumor, and I returned to India to be with him. I told him about the branch manager job in San Diego.

"Mayur, you know that I have never stopped you from doing anything you truly wanted to do," my father said, "but I'm asking you to please reject this branch manager position. Instead, build a business model around your true gift: the caring, wise way you have guided and interacted with all of your family members, including me. Our family will be strong for generations because of your leadership. Guide other families toward being strong as well. They need your insight. They need your life experience. They need your help."

My father then told me that he knew his time was almost up; that he was not going to make it. With tears in his eyes, he handed me a stack of old letters. He explained that he had kept every letter I'd ever written to him from the time I was eight-years old. He told me how proud he was of me and how much he loved me. Then he uttered the words I had been waiting my entire life to hear:

Now, everybody knows me as your father.

And at that moment he made me "head of the household," meaning that from then on I would be responsible for the emotional, spiritual, physical and financial well-being of each of our family members.

I was 38-years old.

I took to heart my father's mandate to help other families. As soon as I returned home following his death, I resigned my manager position and started my own financial services practice, The Legacy Planning Group, Inc., in 1997 with the overarching theme of "Saving and Empowering Families for Generations."

What pushed me this far in business was not my intellect and ambition alone. It was also my grandfather's and my father's steadfast faith in me. It was their wisdom, their vision, and their direction that laid the foundation for everything I've built.

Despite their struggles, my grandfather and father also experienced moments of great financial success, yet I never felt entitled to anything.

Because they passed on their insights and high standards with such love and skill, they inspired me to constantly reach higher and do more. This has become their legacy to me and to the generations that have followed them up to now. This will be their gift to their descendants far into the future.

I thought I was left alone to build my road map after I lost my grandfather and father, but God helped me find new levels of support. I was very fortunate and blessed when I was introduced in one year to four extraordinary people.

The first was Dan Sullivan, co-founder of an outstanding organization called Strategic Coach. Dan helps entrepreneurs succeed by thinking and doing outside their comfort zone. I am so grateful to him for challenging me to build my unique process and the intellectual capital it takes to set myself apart from the thousands of other advisors out there, and for helping me achieve an unfair advantage. His coaching also helped me ask right the questions and develop a methodology which transformed me from being a good estate planner to a respected thought leader. He also surrounded me with several other successful business owners who gave me hope and also reassurance because they had been down this path before. This extraordinary ecosystem gave me courage, confidence and comfort, which ultimately empowered me to become the absolute best I can be.

- The second new supportive relationship was the Enlightened Spiritual Leader HDH Pramukh Swami Maharaj. Pujya Swamibapa, as we affectionately call him, has inspired millions of his devotees through his humility, empathy, compassion and care, and he has made world better place. On the very first day I met him in August 1998 and he held my hands in his, I felt unconditional love and the purity of his heart. He looked me in the eye and asked if he were to request something from me, would I help? When I took out my checkbook, he told me he was not asking for money. What he needed was my life experience and expertise. The next day I was entrusted by him to help the Hindu organization Bochansanwasi Akshar Purushottam Swaminarayan Sanstha (BAPS) share its message of peace and harmony throughout the USA by building temples and community centers around the world, empowering their volunteer leaders with donor relationship management, and increasing awareness as well as engagement of the mainstream.

Pujya Swamibapa spent countless hours with me, guiding me and blessing me with the confidence that God will make it happen. He just happen to be guiding light. His wisdom to me was

- **"You are not the creator , you are medium through which thoughts and actions flow"**

- **Humility : Higher up you go, more Humble you become**

I experienced his humility personally when, after eight long hours meeting in Gondal, India, he took me by the hand and led me to Holy Temple where we did offer our prayers (circling a shrine or other sacred object) around Akshar Deri. As we walked purposefully around the sacred site 11 times, Pujya Swamibapa explained to me—in front of pictures of his Gurus/Teachers Bhagatji Maharaj, Shastriji Maharaj and Yogiji Maharaj—that his Gurus inspire him, his devotees do all the hard work; that he does not actually do anything. In reality, Pujya Swamibapa worked tirelessly 18 hours a day, 365 days a year meeting 500 people every day and answering 100 letters every day in addition to overseeing the organization's worldeide activities. Yet still he felt so light! It was amazing to witness. In fact, during the eight hours we met that day (along with Pujya Vivek sagar Swami and Pujya Brahmvihari Swami) I experienced his clarity, brilliance, wisdom and attention to details along with time management skills that I had not seen in another human being in my lifetime. As our time came to a close, he told me he had full confidence in me and that he would be with me every step of the way. I felt so blessed. I joyfully took upon the responsibility of serving him to make the world a better place.

Atamaswarup Swami (then head of the London Temple and subsequently head of Akshardham Temple New Delhi) and Pujya Yagnavallabh Swami (head saint of North America) were constantly giving me valuable input in addition to Swamishri's guidance. For four years from 1999-2003, I had an extraordinary journey during which I balanced managing my practice with travelling around the country and serving Swamibapa for his mission to improve the world and the community. With his Blessings and selfless sacrifice from thousands of his devotees, we have six shrine Temples in Chicago, Houston, Atlanta, Los Angeles, Robbinsville, New Jersey and Toronto, along with 90 others around the USA and Canada to promote a message of peace, family harmony and an addiction-free society.

In 2000 Pujya Swamibapa asked me to establish BAPS CARE, now known as BAPS Charities, to support civics, health, education, relief work and leadership development. Volunteers of BAPS Charities have helped in the aftermath of the San Francisco earthquake, Hurricane Katrina, the Gujarat earthquake, the tsunami in Japan and various floods around the world.

Every Sunday young people from age five to 30 are given opportunities to learn and participate in self-development. And every year in America there are week-long summer retreats for youth—planned and implemented by youth—for 3,000-plus people… and these retreats are flawless! He has created a sustainable system for preserving values amongst younger generations and keeping all ageless traditions of sharing wisdom alive through Sunday afternoon assembly where millions attend worldwide to serve, share and grow selflessly!

By impacting all generations this way, Pujya Swamibapa has not only taught me but showed me that his actions are louder than words. He has inspired over 1,000 learned youth in the last 70 years to renounce life's comforts and adopt celibacy to serve millions of his devotees throughout 50 countries.

He gave me a mandate during the inauguration of the Akshardham New Delhi Temple in 2002 when he said,

"Mayur, what I am doing in saffron clothes of impacting families and preserving values, you have to do in white clothes. Save the generations and promote the transfer of family values and wisdom from generation to generation."

This was the reinforcement of my grandfather's and father's mandate. I knew at that time it was my calling.

Swamibapa left this world on august 13, 2016 at 96-years of age , and even now he continues to guide me and my family on every issue in divine form. After my grandfather and father he has impacted me the most by making me transform myself and helping me scale my emotional and spiritual capacity to serve. I am forever indebted to him for the difference he has made in my life.

To illustrate what I mean, I would like to share two stories that impacted me over my 18 years with him.

Many years ago we had major tragedy in our family. My niece (my sister's daughter) lost her husband and two other members of her husband's family in a car accident within one year of their wedding. The entire family was emotionally devastated and looking for solace and direction. My sister and brother-in-law talked to me about it. Consequently I requested Swamiji to guide my brother-in-law. Swamiji spent over 30 minutes on the phone with him even though they had never met.

He not only comforted my brother-in-law but also gave him insight that the journey of life has both birth and death as an integral part. The soul leaves the body and therefore the soul is immortal. We have to celebrate the life of the person who departed and talk about all the good deeds the person did rather than mourning the loss. When you accept death with the same level of joy you have when a child arrives in world, you have accomplished the state of co-existence with the body and soul. To this day—15 years later—my brother-in-law still carries Swamiji's words from that conversation in his heart along with the understood wisdom that the soul never dies; only the body is mortal. Death is a celebration of life and not the end of life. We must never feel sorry for the suffering… in fact we should pray to whichever god we worship and ask him to provide strength and courage to face our adversities.

The second story deals with my son and daughter.

In 2007 when my son, Sagar, was studying at the University of Michigan, Swamiji made a trip to the USA and called Sagar to Houston. There he spent 30 minute with my son offering guidance for his future professional career, but emphasizing one fact very clearly: never trade family values for financial progress. Take care of family first, and always show your compassion for others.

Swamiji also helped my daughter. Even though Reema was accepted to prestigious Medical School, she had it in her heart to pursue business. Through me, Swamiji guided her to follow her passion, pointing out that it is not a medical degree that helps in life but rather being a visionary and a clear thinker. As a result, my daughter summoned the courage to pursue her business idea.

In life we are presented with so many choices. It helps to have someone you can count on to assist you in developing a high level of clarity and the confidence to take decisive actions. My entire family has benefited from this spiritual journey with HDH Swamibapa and all his saints.

In addition to Dan Sullivan and Swamibapa, I also met two other men who brought a positive impact to my life: Scott Fithian and Bill Bachrach, whose work helped financial advisors build practices around values-based planning. Bill and Scott helped me fine-tune my approach to values-based planning to create a roadmap for community and client impact. Scott and I resonated instantly, We had great decade together in evolving values based planning methodogy that became game changer to Financial services industry. I express my gratitude to scott to formalize and memorialize Values based philosophy for every family and achieve better clarity as well as emotional freedom to make well informed life choices.

Unfortunately I lost my friend Scott in 2006 to cancer. Still, I have continued the journey of saving families and impacting generations through our work on creating unique 100-year road maps. Scott's four-quadrant approach to values-based legacy planning and business succession planning helped me customize my own approach with the 65 client families we serve today.

Legacy Perpetuator Process™

MISSION, VISION, VALUES & GOALS
WHAT planning gaps are we trying to close and WHY ?

CONFODENCE
Results Management
Leading to Confidence

CLARITY
Discovery Leading
to Clarity

RESULTS MANAGEMENT

DISCOVERY

4 Sustain
The Result

1 Identify
Vision & Goals

THE PLANNING HORIZON™

3 Imlpement
The Solution

2 Think About
The Solution

STRATEGY DEPLOMENT

CREATIVE SOLUTIONS

RESULTS
Stretegy Deployment
Leading to Results

DECISIONS
Creative Solutions
Leading to Decisions

STRATEGIGS, TACTICS & TOOLS
WHO will help us close our panning gaps and HOW ?

Scott's emphasis on above-the-line planning focuses on the unique journey of every individual and family. He taught me that when you ask discovery questions to these families it continues to empower them by forcing to them to look within. As their wealth coach we seek to understand their issues, concerns, challenges and opportunities. We help them gain clarity about their future. We help them understand:

- Who are you?

- Why are you here?

- What is your purpose?

- What would you like to be known for while you are here?

The second and third quadrants deal with diagnosing problems and implementation with various products/services. This is what most industry experts focus on. Sustainability is the fourth quadrant, which allows us to help every family stay on track with respect to what matters to them in all their different life stages.

I tell you these stories of my grandfather, my father, Dan, Swamiji, Scott and Bill because they were my inspiration for creating the reason for this book Achieve Emotional Freedom. Share your wisdom, vision and unique abilities and grow your family's emotional, spiritual, relational and financial wealth… by design and on purpose. As my friend Dan Sullivan is so fond of saying, you will experience "10X growth" in every facet of your life, including family harmony, when you follow the prescription outlined here.

This book is an experiential and exploratory journey for you and your loved ones. By following this process you can transform from being a dysfunctional family to a harmonious family. You can go from having stagnant relationships to fantastic mutually-collaborative relationships. And you and your loved ones can grow tenfold in your pursuit of personal, professional and financial wellbeing, not because you **have to,** but because you truly **want to** !

Chapter 2:

Plotting the Course for a Multi-Generational Roadmap

> *Today we are blessed with the goodness of our hearts, but we are cursed by an environment that distracts us from what matters most.*
>
> *Let us clear a path so our hearts can lead us forward.*

You are probably reading this book because you are thinking about your future. Your thoughts might wander, but will likely touch on subjects like your financial security and well-being, your family, your values, your faith and the sum total of your life's work. You question how your life has made a difference in the world. You imagine the legacy you are planning to leave, and you worry about your family's sustainability. Perhaps your family is not as strong a unit as you would like it to be due to some unresolved conflicts.

You may believe family harmony is not possible for you and yours, but I promise you that it is. We have coached scores of affluent families through a process of discovering, evaluating, implementing and sustaining their legacies, and we know it is achievable for any family that's truly willing. The process and tools we have developed help people clarify and share their most important beliefs, values and wisdom about life, career, family and money with the generations that follow. It helps them understand why they've made certain decisions about the ultimate distribution of their wealth. It allows them to express their hope that the younger generations will participate with them in life and also succeed them in saving, spending and sharing their wealth in a manner congruent with their life principles.

Every family has its own outlook and situation, including yours. Some are doing pretty well and simply want to fine-tune their family harmony. Some are dealing with an imbalance between their business and their family, and they need equilibrium. Others have children or grandchildren who are extraordinarily bright but are completely alienated from their elders' values, and they want to bring the young ones back into the fold before it's too late. That's why the coaching protocol we've created is fully customizable to meet each family's unique needs. But even though our method's got a lot of flexibility, it always begins at the beginning… with Discovery.

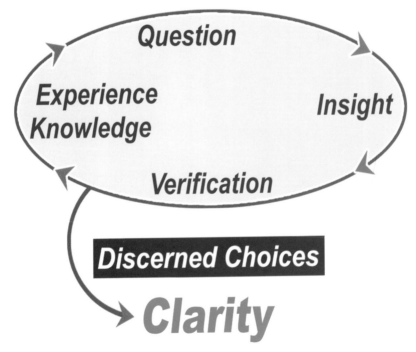

The "Inner View"

Very few people ever get to bottom of what is preventing them from taking their life to the next level because they haven't been able to break through the barriers to their psyche. For that reason we call the heart of our Discovery process not an interview but an inner view. This is not about how much I know as a professional coach. It is not about how good I am at giving advice. It is all about you. We ask targeted questions about your unique journey; questions that help you uncover and celebrate your best qualities while simultaneously bringing to light those things that may be holding you back. The more questions we ask the better we are able to focus on all your concerns and challenges, helping you crystalize and then realize what is important to you. As we guide you toward discovering who you are, we direct your attention not only on where you have been but also where you want to be as an individual and as a family leader. Our whole purpose is to help you carve out a positive future for your business and your family, two generations or more down the line.

During this inner view process we use a variety of questionnaires and surveys that promote deep reflection. Who made the greatest impact in your life during your formative years and into adulthood? How did this person/these people influence your experience as a child and as a young adult? Who helped you become focused on doing what you do now? Which priceless values did you pick up from your parents, grandparents, mentors, teachers and others around you? What kind of environment shaped you? What is the most significant gift you've ever received; the gift that most contributed to who you are today? What is the most significant gift you've ever given? These are the types of questions we ask using a series of in-depth inquiry tools we've developed over decades of coaching affluent families through the process of creating customized family succession plans.

Human Capital of Family

Are we managing our financial capital in such away that it is at the service of the human capital ?

* Are future generations prepared to inherit and manage the wealth ?
* Are they prepared to act responsibly ?

* What values are important to our family and how can we be sure they are sustained across generations ?

Do we have a mission and purpose for the wealth that is clearly understood and accepted across the family ?

* Are we mentoring each generation so that older generations can serve as role models for younger family members ?

Family Governance Issues

#1
* Is the family better off separating into separate branches or staying together ?
* Do we have clear decision making mechanisms in the family ?

#2
* Have we set a series of policies that can help frame challenging decisions we need to make across different family members ?
* Have we developed effective conflict resolution mechanism

#3
* Have we focused on succession planing ?
* Have we done scenario planning in case of unexpected events or crisis ?

The process applies to all families . Every one of them has had a unique journey. Every one of them has the capacity to create an amazing impact in their households and in the world at large

One of the most momentous truths about everyone—whether they are leading a thriving start-up company, whether they are significant wealth holders, or whether they are homemakers who have fulfilled the extraordinary role of raising children who turn out to be successful—is that the sacrifice of one person can transform the lives of many.

I recall family from a 26 years ago, a gentleman in his 50s who had trained and mentored hundreds of pediatricians in America, impacting dozens of his family members future met me at social event . This gentleman was the kind of person that everyone holds up as an example of humility and service. Of him they all say, "When we needed him, he was there." He seeked our help to develop road map to share his values and virtues for his future generations.

I spent 20 hours engaged in the Discovery process with him, listening to him explain his unique journey and to uncover his deeper purpose for this lifetime. At one point he recalled a lesson his uncle had taught him when he was young, which was that most people are focused on their own self-interest above all else. If you can do one little thing to feed the self-interest of each person you encounter then you can make that person's life better. It doesn't have to be huge or time consuming, but it does have to be genuine. By doing so you can give them a sense of belonging and connection, if only for a moment. His uncle taught him that when you do that, you get something beautiful in return... you get a sense of satisfaction and meaning that you can't get any other way.

I encouraged my client to renew his commitment to personifying his uncle's lesson. He made the choice to do so and quickly discovered that the more he engaged in this practice, the wider and more positive his circle of influence became. His benevolence was like a happy ripple on a lovely pond, radiating goodwill ever outward and becoming magnified through each person he touched. Once my client had achieved this tremendous insight, there was nothing stopping him. He proceeded to move mountains personally and professionally. Remember, this gentleman was in his late 50s at the time we conducted his inner view. He is living proof that wisdom is ageless.

In most cases the Discovery I've described here is conducted with all members of the family, which I call G1, G2 and G3 stakeholders ("G" standing for generation). Since each generation has its own unique set of strengths and challenges, each one is provided with its own unique set of questionnaires and surveys to complete prior to our individual and family meetings. Bringing everyone to the table singularly and later as a group results in profound life experiences. Discovery helps you develop a family philosophy, a shared vision and a collective knowledge that provides clarity about where you are going as individuals and as a group. It brings to light any gaps that exist between where you are now and where you want to be tomorrow and years from now. And it helps develop a new set of choices that will positively affect everyone in the family whose life you want to impact. The new family philosophy essentially provides a governance structure to support you going forward.

By examining the past, you identify what your family/business traditions and values were all about. By analyzing your place in the present, you are provided with context and the freedom to think rather than just feel and react. And finally, developing a snapshot of the future you hope to create provides you with inspiration because your energy is focused on making tomorrow better than today.

Discovery, discovery and more discovery. This is what life—and passing on a legacy of wealth and wisdom—is all about.

Evaluation, Implementation and Sustainability

Let's imagine that you and your family have just engaged in a phase of Discovery. To get you all moving forward, we then conduct an analysis of your inner view and offer solutions for growth and change. Once your choices are clear we help you cherry-pick what is important to you, and we walk alongside you as you implement and exercise your options. As a result you are empowered with a high level of comfort because nobody else has made those decisions for you. You have made them. When you make decisions, you own them. And once you own your decisions, your confidence and courage soar. Speaking the truth becomes natural for you. Sharing the story of who you are and why you are here becomes easy. It becomes a way of life for every member of the family.

And when it comes to your wealth, you will be able to share it joyfully and in abundance because you will understand that you are merely a medium through which the resources are passed. During your inner view we crystalized your vision, values and goals, and we will use what we learned to craft a family wealth optimization strategy that gives you and all stakeholders ultimate confidence and peace of mind. We'll then develop a system to ensure ongoing review of your wealth optimization strategy's progress.

Every relationship you have will truly benefit from your insight, your generous spirit and your wisdom in having undertaken this process. So too will the world benefit, because you will have refined your family's approach to philanthropy to ensure that you are making the greatest impact in the areas you care about most.

Again, the work we do in all four stages—discovery, evaluation, implementation and sustainability—is customized to match each family's unique outlook and needs. For some the emphasis will be on simply fine-tuning family harmony. For others it will be about improving the balance between running the business and nurturing the generations. For others, it will be about creating a succession plan. Still others have extraordinarily bright children who are completely alienated from their elders' values; in this case the entire family requires mentoring, coaching about their non-financial wealth, and help dealing with issues pertinent to bringing the younger ones into the circle. But in all cases the ultimate goal is establishing total clarity in every aspect of the family's life, in each and every person.

Once you create that level of clarity in a person, whether they are a teenage grandchild or a 75-year old grandfather like the client I told you about a moment ago, then that person will feel comfortable inviting others into their life in an authentic way. They will feel comfortable switching roles and mentoring others with empathy and complete humility. They will turn away from attachment and develop an inner core of detachment. When one's inner core is filled with detachment, they no longer feel entitlement driven. They no longer feel anxious about their expectations not being met because they have no expectations. They no longer will feel like a victim. They are now ready to say to each and every member of the family, "Thank you for being part of my life. Thank you for walking along with me."

This is how you can achieve the sustainability of your wisdom, values, business savvy and family best practices. This is how you find out who you are as individuals and as a family. This is how you all stand up together and declare what you want to be known for, now and far into the future.

If you are best in class in your industry (whether it is medicine, hospitality, jewelry, technology, philanthropy… whatever work you do) ask yourself this question: am I as good in every other part of my life? If the answer to that question is "no," wouldn't you love to become better? And if the answer is "yes," wouldn't you love to become better than best?

This is your opportunity. This is what sustainability is all about.

And now let's explore how our process of discovery, evaluation, implementation and sustainability helped three affluent families share their wealth and wisdom to grow meaningful and secure futures for the next generations. These families are fictional of course, but their case studies contain facets of actual coaching clients we've been able to help over the past several decades. Each family has different issues that need to be addressed. They all have a different emotional mindset and readiness to implement. If you were to look collectively at the three families, you would see that the process and the methodology we used with them are basically the same, but the outcomes are very different. The insights are profound for each family as we work to get them to understand exactly what they are doing in their lives.

You will likely recognize bits and pieces of your own reality in the pages that follow. If that's the case, I pray that the examples presented here serve as comforting proof that you are not alone. I pray that you find hope in the stories I'm imparting to you. And I pray that you will be inspired to undertake your own Legacy Perpetuator™ process so that your family can share and grow, too… together and in harmony.

MEHTA FAMILY

A Family That *Thinks* They Know
What They Know

SMITH FAMILY

A Family That Knows
What They Don't Know

CORDERO FAMILY

A Family That Doesn't Know,
What They Don't Know

Let us
Being our Journey
together

PART 2:
THE MEHTA'S

A Family That *Thinks* They Know What *They Know*

Chapter 3:

Meet the Mehta's

Your mindset is not something you are born with,
Your mindset is a choice.

By all outward appearances, the Mehta's had it all. The family patriarch, Raj Mehta, was a renowned neurosurgeon practicing at one of the most prestigious medical centers in the country. The matriarch, Mina, was a highly-regarded psychiatrist whose research was often cited in scholarly journals. Their adult son, Jay, owned a graphic design company and their daughter, Tanya, was a successful consultant. All told, the Mehta's were a smart, ambitious family whose members took great pride in their careers and their standing in the community.

When I first met Raj and Mina, they were in their late-60s and beginning to wind down their careers. Still enjoying good physical health and with a net worth of close to $50 million, you'd think they would have been optimistic about their family's future. Nothing could have been further from the truth. Both husband and wife were deeply troubled by the lack of harmony in their relationships, not only with one another but also between them and their children. The relationship between Raj and Jay was especially strained. Raj blamed the conflict on his son's "entitlement attitude" while Jay expressed frustration with his father's inability to give a gift without strings attached. Mina, always caught in the middle, had no idea how to navigate the minefield created by her husband and son. And although she was a smart woman, Mina felt like an intellectual lightweight next to her husband, whose brain power was legendary. Raj did nothing to reassure his wife that he valued her intellect and opinion; in fact, he sometimes exploited his superior intelligence.

In light of all this upheaval, Jay had distanced himself—literally—by moving 1,500 miles away from his parents, returning to the family home only for occasional holidays, weddings and funerals. The couple's daughter, Tanya, lived nearby with her husband Mark, their daughter Kyra and son Anay; her relationship with her parents was cordial but somewhat superficial.

Unfortunately, family discord was nothing new for the Mehta's. Raj and Mina had been married for over 40 years after having met in college, but they'd never been able to get their act together at home. They'd sought advice from a variety of counselors and coaches and had attended numerous self-help seminars and events over the years. Afterward they would experience momentary peace, but it never lasted. That's because they had taken away nuggets of good advice from the experts they'd consulted but they had not shifted their mindsets. They'd practiced a patchwork type of recovery by attempting to treat the symptoms without first identifying the disease.

And now, as Raj and Mina prepared for retirement and considered what would become of the wealth and wisdom they'd amassed over their lifetimes, they were genuinely afraid. They worried that the younger generations in their family were not prepared to handle the fortune they'd be leaving behind. They had no idea how to effectively pass on their values and wisdom to their children and grandchildren, and they knew time was slipping away. In a nutshell, their hearts were broken because they could not see a pathway to creating and leaving a legacy that would matter.

In our initial consultation, the Mehta's expressed skepticism about their chances for getting better because they'd "failed" so many times in the past. But I assured them that our way was different. We would be using our unique four-part process to drill down deeply; to discover and evaluate the underlying sources of their challenges as individuals, as a couple and as a family. We'd then implement a series of recommendations based on our discovery and evaluation, and we'd work together to develop a formal family governance protocol to guide them and their descendants into the future—together—in a positive way. The result of all our efforts would be a 100-year roadmap to sustain their success for generations to come.

Despite Raj and Mina's initial cynicism, they agreed to give our process a try.

"What have we got to lose?" Raj said with a shrug. "Our situation can't get much worse, that's for sure."

The Mehta's Discovery Begins

After only a short time talking with the patriarch and matriarch of the Mehta family, it became clear to me that they were suffering from three profound challenges common among affluent families:

- **Lack of empathy for one another, leading to a victim mentality among all stakeholders.**

- **Lack of full engagement with each other, leading to an absence of transparency when it came to sharing their concerns, challenges, vision, mission and purpose as a couple and as a family.**

- **Lack of clarity about the true sources of their joy and happiness, leading them to erupt like volcanoes over the small stuff.**

The more we talked, the more I learned about their dysfunctional approach to solving problems. The family's common M.O. over the last 40 years was to form alliances amongst themselves to try to force the odd man out to do whatever it was they wanted. For example, when Raj and one of the children butted heads, Mina and the kids would form an alliance against Raj. Sometimes the kids and Raj ganged up on Mina. Sometimes the parents pitted the children against one another. Raj and Mina had no unified vision. They coexisted but rarely collaborated. They were intellectually capable but emotionally fragile... and to complicate matters, they both had massive egos.

To establish a benchmark for the family's recovery, we used a tool called the Harmony Scorecard to assess their current state of family unity. With a harmony score of only 25%, it was obvious that we had a lot of work to do.

Completed Harmony Scorecard for "Mehta's"

Initial ◆25

After 3 years ◆75

We began the Discovery segment of our process by having Raj and Mina fill out a Living Legacy Questionnaire, which revealed some interesting truths about their childhoods. First their similarities: both Raj and Mina came from households with cautious spenders. Neither were allowed to handle money when they were young. Both sets of parents instilled a strong work ethic and love of family in their children, and their top priorities were education and integrity. The questionnaire also revealed some striking differences between Raj and Mina's early years. Raj was the second child in a family of ten kids; he was also the firstborn son. His mother controlled the family's money. Raj's parents encouraged independent thinking, but his father was very assertive as long as he was paying. There was a great deal of discord between Raj's parents, causing much stress in the household. They were not a religious family.

On the other hand, Mina's family was very religious. She was the fourth of six kids. Sadly, her mother had passed away when Mina was 12, and she was raised by an older sister. Consequently she was taught to be strong and not cause any trouble. Her father, a smart and hard-working man, handled his family's finances. Saving was important to him, not only for the future but also to contribute to religious causes.

The next part of the Living Legacy Questionnaire focused on Raj and Mina's values as adults. Again, some interesting insights were gained as we ranked each person's most and least important values. They discovered (much to their delight) that they shared many of the same ideals: attention to emotional health, physical health and family relationships. Among their least important values was a need for solitude. Both indicated that they craved intimacy and connection with one another.

We then asked Raj to reflect on his wife and describe his feelings about her. He said he loved that he and Mina shared the same core values, and he was very confident in her ability to handle money. When it was Mina's turn to describe her feelings about her husband, she replied that they shared many similarities (persistence, love, intelligence, confidence) but that sometimes their egos got in the way. She made special note of the fact that her husband was much more intelligent than she… more on that later.

The next segment of the Discovery process delved into the couple's feelings about their children, Jay and Tanya; their son-in-law, Mark; and their grandchildren, Kyra and Anay. Raj and Mina said their kids were smart people and they had confidence in Tanya's ability to manage wealth. However, they were worried about Jay's capabilities in that regard because they feared he might overspend. As for Mark, both Raj and Mina expressed their admiration for their son-in-law and fully expected that their relationship with him would only deepen as the years passed. And when asked to reflect on their grandchildren, the Mehta's said they had no major concerns there. Their joint wish was that Kyra and Anay would grow to be educated, happy, honest, successful, kind and loving people, and they had every reason to believe that this would be the outcome. The grandkids were doing well, and Mark and Tanya were good parents.

Next we asked the Mehta's to name the universal principle holding their family together right now. Their response: love. Then we asked them to think about their family in the future. What would they like to see happen in the next three years? Raj replied that he'd like greater bonding among the family members and more open communication. Mina said practically the same thing—she'd like more closeness and honest communication about the good and the bad within their family.

(As we analyzed their responses, we couldn't help but notice how much in alignment this couple was when it came to what they wanted out of life. Why, then, were they so unhappy? We knew the answer would present itself if we only kept digging.)

Then we examined the Mehta's reflections on money. Raj and Mina agreed that they would need $350,000 annually to live as they were accustomed. They also agreed that not only did they want to leave an inheritance to their descendants, they also wanted to continue their philanthropic efforts into the future. They identified the causes and charities they'd most like to support—those helping children, women and girls; and education, the arts and medicine. It was good to see that they were in solid accord on their finances.

We also asked questions to assess Raj and Mina's health and physical lives. Again there were similarities between the two. Both were healthy and expected to live several more decades. They had the proper end-of-life paperwork in place (living wills, power of attorney, testamentary wills and donor-directed trusts) and they had discussed their final wishes with one another. Raj had also discussed his final wishes with the kids, but Mina had not. We urged her to do so without delay.

Moving on, we asked the Mehta's to reflect on their careers. Raj said that his work as a neurosurgeon had taught him a lot about life; chiefly that you have to love what you do and that humility is essential to your success, both professionally and personally. He loved serving his patients and he suffered greatly on the sad occasions when someone was beyond his help. He confided that his greatest concern about passing on his wealth was how to turn it over to the next generation without them losing their creativity and spirit. We assured him that the process we were undertaking would help make that possible.

We then turned to Mina's feelings about her career. She said her work had taught her that persistence, honesty and communication would always generate success, and money would come by having integrity both professionally and personally. She said her biggest career challenge was dealing effectively with the administrators of her organization. Her greatest concerns were being able to construct a sound inheritance plan, and also how to spend their money not only meeting the family's needs but also supporting charities that reflected her values.

Finally, we asked Raj and Mina to think about their life's purpose. Raj responded that his purpose in life was to inspire people. He cited his weekly volunteer work teaching math to Highschool students as helping him fulfill his purpose. He wrote that while he considered himself good at solving complex problems, he was "drained" by the lack of harmony with his wife. Not being able to resolve that fundamental challenge was holding him back from feeling that he had truly fulfilled his life's purpose. When asked what he would like engraved on a plaque in his honor, he said, "Raj was a man who enjoyed his life and brought smiles to many."

The same was true for Mina, who said that her purpose was "to live happily and spread happiness." Toward that end she treasured her time traveling, creating art and playing with the grandchildren. But she confessed that family disagreements posed a constant threat to the fulfillment of her purpose. For the inscription on her plaque, Mina said, "She thanks her husband for teaching her about life and philanthropy."

By the time we finished reviewing the couples' responses to our Living Legacy Questionnaire, we had a much better idea of who they and their offspring were, what was important to them, and what their strengths and challenges were. We could now begin digging deeper in a search for the diamonds and gold we knew were within the Mehta's as individuals and as a family.

At this point we set up a series of weekly phone counseling sessions we refer to as Family Governance Calls. Sometimes the calls are conducted on an individual basis and sometimes they are joint, with both husband and wife on the phone with me.

I'll never forget the first of the many joint calls I had with the Mehta's. Raj and Mina were preparing for a trip to visit Jay a few days later, to see for the first time the home they had recently bought for him and to celebrate his 35th birthday. The last time they'd spoken, Raj and Jay had argued about interest Jay was supposed to pay on a promissory note, and the matter was still not settled. So while the Mehta's were eager to see their son and his new home, they also had trepidations about whether they'd be able to make it through their two-day stay without a quarrel.

As food for thought before their trip, I asked Raj and Mina to listen very carefully to my words over the next several minutes, and to meditate on them afterward. Here is what I told them...

Chapter 4:

Thirteen Toxic Energies

*To be Happy, Change what You can and
Accept what you have no control over.*

Most of us go through life not intending to hurt anyone, least of all our family members. But unfortunately our intentions don't always match our reality. Family members—especially those in families like yours with significant wealth—very often do hurt one another. I think that's because there's a lack of clarity, consciousness and courage in many of today's most affluent families. Without clarity, consciousness and courage, healthy relationships cannot be sustained.

Let's imagine that you are the head of a family and I am a member of the second generation. If you feel hurt because of certain things I've done and I am not consciously aware of your pain, I will probably continue to hurt you. You will continue to hold a low opinion of me based on your personal experience and observation. Your entire expectation management for our relationship will change. You are not going to treat me with the same level of trust and empathy as before. Instead you will conduct your relationship with me not as mutually interdependent, but as transactional. In a transactional relationship, "Who cares?" becomes the formula, and "Why should I worry?" becomes the attitude. Once that formula and that attitude are present, the entire family is in danger of self-destructing.

It takes 25-years to build a generation, but it only takes 25-weeks to destroy one. If someone is hypercritical of you week after week, do you think you will give them the opportunity to be part of your life after 26-weeks? Probably not. The relationship is likely destroyed for a generation.

On the other hand, if the wise head of the family (or any insightful person in the family, for that matter) can achieve clarity and summon the courage to reach out to the self-serving ones and help them understand how their behavior threatens the longevity and sustainability of everything the patriarch and matriarch have created, then the family can be preserved. Clarity, courage and conscious awareness are instrumental in preserving the family and saving the generation.

But it's not only the younger generation's actions that threaten family ties. In many cases the younger generation sees the elders as unable or unwilling to relinquish any control whatsoever. Usually this is because the elders are striving to protect the wealth of the younger generation, which is a noble and reasonable desire. But what the elders fail to understand is that the younger members of the family think differently than they do. The younger ones may be quick learners who could achieve positive life-changing results if given the opportunity. They need freedom and space to grow, and if they are properly engaged they can move mountains. They can transform themselves and sustain the family and its wealth far into the future. Sadly they are not always given the chance.

Indeed, one of the single most poisonous attitudes affecting the sustainability of the family is the patriarch's and/or matriarch's mistaken assertion that they are always right. Their thinking goes something like this: *I am the wealth holder, so the others need to change and get around me. If the young ones do not listen to me, I am not going to do anything for them.*

The younger generation's response is that their parents' or grandparents' hard work and luck do not give them the exclusive right to behave as a scolding CEO all the time. This gap in understanding leads to tremendous amounts of resentment and apathy, and an absence of closeness and effectiveness at home.

Another thing that leads to resentment and an absence of closeness in the family is the patriarch and matriarch's failure to form a cohesive unit against all outside relationships, including their relationships with the children. Visualize a triangle with each line in the triangle representing a person, independent but connected to the other two. A respectful balance has to be maintained in order to keep that triangle whole. This translates into not focusing solely on who is "right" and being careful to only give an opinion or answer when it can be backed up by knowledge or concrete facts.

Then I shared with Raj and Mina the 13 toxic energies in our lives that prevent us from performing at the highest level as individuals and as family members:

13 Toxic Energies

1.	**Stubbornness**	:	*I am right, and I will not consider any alternative.*
2.	**Attention-seeking**	:	*I will do whatever it takes to get you to notice me, even if it hurts me or you.*
3.	**Jealousy**	:	*Instead of focusing on my own capacity for growth, I'd rather resent other people's progress and achievement.*
4.	**Apathy**	:	*I don't care one way or the other. I am completely indifferent.*
5.	**Fault finding**	:	*If you'd only improve on your weaknesses, you'd be a better person.*
6.	**Anger**	:	*If things don't go my way, I will explode like a pressure cooker!*
7.	**Lust**	:	*I want what I want, and I want it NOW.*
8.	**Expectations**	:	*Why must you people constantly disappoint me?*

9. Greed	:	*I don't care if I already have plenty of (wealth, power, love, food)… I want MORE.*
10. Attachment	:	*My bond with thisbusiness and/or family which I have created is so strong that it prevents me from thinking clearly. I get deeply upset if anything or anyone threatens it.*
11. Desire	:	*I want this (thing or person) with all my heart. I want it so badly that my judgment becomes clouded, but that's OK… my desire is the only thing that matters.*
12. Ego	:	*I did all this for you, so you'd better acknowledge and respect me.*
13. Selfishness	:	*Hey, what's in it for me? What's mine is mine and what's yours is mine! I deserve it and I'm going to have it.*

These toxic energies endanger everything you and your family have built. Your family cannot be expected to grow **emotionally, spiritually,** or in **relationship** with one another if these poisonous energies are present, nor can the people within it be expected to sustain good **physical health.** And when these four essential elements-emotion, spirit, relationship, and health-are threatened, what happens to the wealth you have accumulated? It goes onto the back burner, and the preservation and transfer of your family's fortune is compromised. This is a truly frightening prospect, but you can liberate yourself and your family if you open your mind and get strategic about confronting these toxic energies.

Chapter 5:

The Antidote to Toxicity

When you accept .your loved ones the way they are,
you unlock the door to family harmony.

The foundation of a strong family is built upon some basic expectations: the expectation of humility from the patriarch and matriarch; the expectation of acceptance by the second and third generations that they have much to learn from their elders' values and best practices; the expectation that all parties will achieve and maintain a positive mindset; the expectation that everyone in the family—regardless of their age and experience—has something of value to contribute; and finally, the expectation that individual and family growth are worthwhile pursuits.

Your family members are more likely to fulfill these expectations when you infuse the environment with four fundamental virtues:

- ◆ Empathy

- ◆ Empowerment

- ◆ Inspiration

- ◆ Clarity

When these virtues are applied consistently within your family, it's like an airplane flying with a strong tailwind. It's time to soar! You will experience exponential growth in terms of harmony, spiritual depth, physical health and financial well-being. That's because your family will become values - driven. Your individual mindsets willbegin to shift from a place of "What's in it for me?" to a place of sharing, caring and growing as a cohesive unit. No longer will family members blame one another for their shortcomings. The victim mentality will disappear as people begin taking full responsibility for their actions. Your collective learning will become organic rather than mechanical, as in $1+1=2$.

There are three bridges that will empower your family to move to this higher, more virtuous level. The first is unwavering faith. When you demonstrate that you have unwavering faith in another person, what you're really demonstrating is total commitment to making your relationship work. You're demonstrating that you trust them completely; that you will always think the best of them and give them the benefit of the doubt. You don't have to create benchmarks to keep track of whether or not they are measuring up to your expectations because there are no expectations... there is only love, good will and faith. When you have that kind of unquestionable faith in another person, it will be reciprocated and the relationship will deepen.

The second bridge is devotion, which, like faith above, is a word most commonly associated with religion. When we go to church, synagogue or Temple, most of us want to join with our fellow worshipers in reciting prayers and being part of the chorus. When we do so, we become immersed in divinity to the point that we forget our own existence, at least for a little while. We're no longer a physician, a CEO or a banker, and neither is the person sitting or kneeling next to us. Nothing matters in that moment except our devotion. The same is true when we're devoted to the members of our family. If I am 100-percent devoted to my son, is the fact that he is a successful attorney relevant to me? Absolutely not. I am devoted to him whether he's a lawyer or whether he's living on the streets.

The opposite of devotion is conditional adjustment of our approval toward another person, which creates lots of challenges and instability in the relationship. When there are strings attached to your approval, trust suffers. But unconditional devotion means that it does not matter how much I have or how much you have. I love you for who you are and what you stand for, period.

The third empowering bridge is gratitude. We are usually only grateful for the good stuff that happens to us, but when you are walking the gratitude bridge with another person your mindset must be this: for whatever you do, I am grateful… even if you are mean to me. Now, why should you be grateful to someone who is mean? The common reaction when we perceive we're being mistreated is to lash out at the other person; to want to teach him or her a lesson. But that reaction will not deepen your relationship or help you grow. When someone is mean to you they are giving you a glimpse into the true meaning of life. They are teaching you what not to do; how not to behave. They are giving you the gifts of enlightenment and perspective, and for that you ought to be profoundly grateful.

Yes, gratitude is a fundamental ingredient in the recipe for a happy life and a happy family, yet when was the last time you saw someone express their gratitude to one who has hurt them? Probably never. People with that depth of gratitude are outliers. Be an outlier. When you are subjected to an adverse circumstance, remember that you have a choice. You can either think, "Oh my God, now what? Why me?" or you can think, "Thank you for this opportunity to grow and to build my strength. Thank you for giving me the courage to confront and overcome this reality. If you come up with any other ways to challenge me, bring them on. I am ready!"

You possess divine power when you react with that sort of total surrender and gratitude. When you walk the three bridges (unwavering faith, devotion and gratitude) with your family members, you will ALL radiate divine power. You will treat one another with loving kindness, and empathy will become your family's greatest virtue.

The True Expression of Empathy:

E =Empowerment

M = Meaning of life

P = Profound gratitude

A = Affection

T = Truth

H = Happiness

Y = Yes, I can. Yes, you can. Yes, WE can.

After I had finished talking about the 13 toxic energies and the three bridges, I asked the Mehta's what kind of birthday gift they planned to give Jay during their trip. They said they had not yet decided. Jay loves fine jewelry and accessories, they said, so they were thinking perhaps a gold watch or diamond cufflinks?

I suggested that Raj and Mina think outside the Tiffany & Co. box this time.

"Why does the gift have to be a store-bought material thing?" I asked. "Why not make something for Jay … something that goes directly from your hearts to his?"

I proposed that the Mehta's create a large photo collage with handwritten messages celebrating all the beautiful ways Jay had blessed the family over the years, and then frame it and present it to their son for his birthday. I asked Raj and Mina to tell me some of the blessings they might include in such a collage. What followed was a tsunami of precious memories: Jay beaming with pride in elementary school after creating a math formula that was far beyond his years... Jay serving as a loving protector for his younger sister Tanya, as he walked her into school on her first day of kindergarten... the great patience and good humor with which he tried (in vain!) to teach his mom how to hit a baseball... Jay bravely setting out on his first cross-country drive as a young adult... planning and starting his own graphic design company... joyously playing tag with his little niece and nephew at the beach last summer... and the list went on and on.

As Raj and Mina spoke these memories, their voices cracked with emotion and their tears fell like rain. They were remembering for the first time in years that their son was more than the sum total of his mistakes; more than just someone who needed to ditch his entitlement attitude and learn to manage money better. As we ended our call, the Mehta's thanked me for the inspiration and said they were confident Jay would be touched and surprised by their gift. They also thanked me for shifting their mindset from fear to hope.

"I feel so much better now that we understand the toxic energies and the three bridges," Mina said. "I actually believe this trip will go well."

Mission accomplished!

Chapter 6:

Stumbling Blocks and Progress

When you become the person you've always wanted to be, you give an immeasurable gift to your family and to the world.

On our next weekly call I asked for an update on how the trip had gone. The Mehta's asked if I wanted the good news or the bad news first. Since I like to start things off on a positive note, I asked for the good news. Mina said that the collage they'd made for Jay was a huge hit; that their son was speechless as he looked at the pictures and read the words his parents had chosen to celebrate his contributions to the family. She said they had a wonderful time together except for the last fifteen minutes of their visit, when Raj brought up the annual interest payments Jay was supposed to make on the promissory note to the trust that had been set up for his benefit. As usual, an argument ensued. Jay said he had not budgeted for the interest payments and didn't understand why he had to pay them at all.

Frustrated, Raj reminded Jay that they had discussed this matter in a phone call only a few weeks prior. The interest was supposed to be paid with the $30,000 they had sent to Jay recently, as recommended by the family's tax advisor... didn't Jay remember Raj explaining it to him over the phone? Jay said he did not remember it that way. Raj demanded to know what had become of the $30,000 earmarked for the interest payment. Jay replied that he had spent it, and then demanded to know why Raj always ruined every visit at the last minute.

As Raj related this story to me, the pain in his voice was obvious.

"It is hard for me to admit this, Mayur, but I fear we have created a trust fund brat," Raj said.

Raj went on to say that Mina had sat in silence during his argument with their son, and he assumed by her facial expression and body language that she was not happy with the way he was handling the situation. I asked Mina to explain her reason for not helping Raj form the cohesive triangle we had discussed on our last call.

"At the time I felt that by staying silent, I was helping Raj," she replied, "but I soon realized that was not so. Where was I? Why didn't I step up? I was equally responsible for the situation with Jay. So as soon as we boarded the plane I apologized to Raj for losing my focus on our new way of being, and he accepted my apology with great kindness."

"We were both culpable," Raj admitted with a sigh. "We fell back on our old ways for a moment, that's all. In hindsight I should have waited until the interest payment was due before bringing it up. This is a steep learning curve for us, Mayur. But honestly, I'm glad the argument happened because we learned a lot. We remembered what you'd told us about being grateful for everything, even the unpleasant things, and on the flight home we talked about how thankful we were to have this opportunity to grow."

It was a good teaching moment for both Raj and Mina. Fragilities are part of life, but now instead of burying them they could learn to deal with them in a way that empowered and liberated their family to move forward with healed wounds rather than festering ones.

As we continued the call we reviewed the actions that had led up to the argument with Jay and brainstormed ways to avoid triggers for similar disputes in the future. I reminded the Mehta's that they cannot seek to make another person's weakness into a strength. It simply doesn't work that way. All discussions with Jay (and everyone else) must point to the positive. Raj and Mina must strive to be active listeners rather than reactive parents. They must never push another down to make a point, nor should they allow anyone to push them down either. I reminded them that when they stand together as a unified entity against outside forces, they are stronger than when each tries to stand alone. I requested that they not share this new "unified front" concept with anyone outside the immediate family, because doing so would only undermine their capacity to work as one.

And so the event with Jay happened, it was discussed, and it was time to move forward and beyond. I was pleased with the Mehta's progress in such a short time, but I knew it was only a baby step in the right direction. They still had a very long way to go toward crafting their wealth mission statement—an expression of their Family Financial Philosophy—which would be the roadmap their advisors would rely on to ensure that all estate planning decisions were consistent with their financial values and objectives. We would also start planning a series of special multi-generational family retreats designed to solidify their beliefs, values and wisdom as individuals, as a couple and as a family. Toward that end we would soon begin including Jay, Tanya and Mark in some of our Family Governance Calls, to begin exposing them to the new mindset and way of being in their family. Jay in particular had more rough edges than Raj and Mina combined, but his parents and I knew he was a smart man. We had every reason to believe that he would realize it was in his best interests to participate fully in the sharing and growing to come.

Still, much patience would be needed. Each stakeholder would require sufficient time to reset their thinking about what it meant to be a member of the Mehta family now, and what it would mean to them in the future. With Raj and Mina setting the pace for the younger generations, they were now ready to move toward crystallizing their beliefs and attitudes about wealth, family and values... together.

Chapter 7:

Mehta Family Update

The challenge is not in finding clarity, it's in sustaining it.

We've now been working with the Mehta's for two years, and both Raj and Mina have had some significant breakthroughs. If you'll recall, Mina lost her mother when she was a pre-teen and she was raised by her elder sister. Because of that unfortunate loss, she's felt like a victim her entire life. But on a recent trip to India to care for the elder sister who was recovering from a major surgery, Mina had an epiphany. One morning she and her sister began talking about the pain of losing their mother. They reminisced about how compassionate and giving their mom was; how her kind and gentle nature filled every corner of every room she entered. At some point during this conversation, the sister reached for Mina's hand and said, "I see our mother in you, Mina; the way you move, the way you speak, the way you share your concern and caring. Of all our mother's children, her compassion lives on the most in you."

In that moment, Mina recalled our counseling sessions about the true meaning of legacy. She realized that for her entire life she had been living off of borrowed wisdom... the wisdom of her sister, her brother and Raj. She'd never staked a claim to what she knows and who she is as a person, and consequently she'd felt terribly frustrated and ineffective in many aspects of her life. But on that day at her sister's bedside she discovered her super power: she had inherited her mother's legacy of compassion, and she would make it her life's purpose to see that this legacy was passed on and sustained. She decided then and there to make her mother live again—through herself—by working to create emotional capacity for her children, Jay and Tanya; to give love and devotion to her grandchildren; personal empathy and gratitude to her son-in-law; and affection, respect and admiration to Raj, her partner in life. She would do this on purpose, by design, intentionally… every day for the remainder of her life. And today she is doing her best. She has never felt more at peace.

Raj, too, has had an epiphany. After witnessing Mina's transformation following the trip to India and becoming the recipient of so much of her empathy and compassion in the weeks that followed, he spoke honestly with us about his own shortcomings. He admitted that he has not always been fully present in his relationship with his wife. He expressed guilt for never helping her around the house. He was ashamed that he had often treated her in a condescending way when she asked questions he considered to be mundane, and he admitted that he had labeled her as "intellectually mediocre" because he happened to have a somewhat quicker mind. He's now trying harder to keep his ego in check. He's making an effort to be much more empathetic and humble by helping Mina in the kitchen and with the laundry, inviting her to take walks with him and treating her with kindness and good humor when she makes a mistake during their weekly bridge games. For once, Raj is having to deal with his wife's superiority at something: her positive personal transformation. He is determined to catch up with her!

The changes in Raj and Mina have not gone unnoticed by their children. A few days after the Mehta's returned from a family retreat to the south of France, we had a Family Governance Call with Jay and Tanya. Raj and Mina were not included because we wanted the kids to be able to speak openly about their retreat experience without having to worry about their parents' reactions. In short, Jay and Tanya told me they were blown away by their father's new-found humility and their mother's positive, peaceful countenance.

"My sister and I are used to Dad throwing his weight around and picking fights with us, and Mom being paranoid and pessimistic about everything," Jay said, "but that was not what we experienced on this trip. It's hard to believe that these are the same two human beings who raised us."

Tanya agreed. She told of a breakthrough moment she and Mina had on the final day of the retreat as they walked together on the beach, just the two of them.

"In all honesty, I've disengaged from Mom over the years because she's kind of a downer," Tanya confided. "But after spending a week with her in France, listening to her stories and watching her interact with Dad and the rest of us, I was stunned by the change in her. I never imagined someone her age could make such a profound transformation, but she has. I wanted to find a way to express how much I admire that. So on the last day she and I were walking on the beach, and I told her how proud I am of her. And I asked her to please tell me what I can do to become worthy of being her daughter. Of course, she cried like a baby after that. We both did."

And then Jay—the "trust fund brat" with an "entitlement mindset"—gave me one of the most satisfying moments I've ever had in all my years doing this work when he chimed in and asked, "Mayur, would it be possible for us to increase the frequency of these calls? There are some things about myself that I want to work on, and I could really use your help."

The Mehta's are changing because they want to change. Nobody is making them do it. Creating a positive impact on the younger generations and the world at large is their choice. They are leaving their old draining experiences behind them and becoming students of life, seeking to purify their thoughts, their sincerity and their compassion. Raj and Mina are making a difference in the lives of their children and grandchildren, who are already beginning to model the behavior of their elders. Consequently everyone in the family feels much happier, calmer and confident.

In fact, on their last Harmony Scorecard—in which Jay, Tanya and Mark participated in addition to Raj and Mina—they scored 75 percent on the Harmony Scale. That's a vast improvement from their initial score of 25 percent. All of them now understand the importance of linking their values and beliefs with their financial objectives. They are already beginning to see the benefits of that, most notably as it relates to Raj and Mina's peace of mind and confidence that the younger generations will be able to handle whatever comes. We are now at the stage where we can begin fine-tuning their financial and wealth transfer plans and setting in motion philanthropic initiatives that truly reflect their values as a family.

The Mehta's know they still have a long path ahead, but thankfully they are well on their way.

PART 3:
THE SMITH'S

A Family That Knows What They Don't Know

Chapter 8:

Meet the Smith's

When you wake up and realize that you are blessed with the capacity to make the world a better place, you don't need anyone's invitation to get started. Simply begin.

I was packing up my briefcase after delivering a presentation about my Legacy Perpetuator™ method at a conference for elite financial planners a few years ago when a gentleman approached me at the podium. "Brian" was a financial planner operating on the West Coast.

"As I listened to you talk today, I couldn't stop thinking about my clients, Dave and Jan Smith," Brian explained. "The Smith's are a great family, but they're dealing with some major stuff right now... serious health concerns, some relationship challenges with the younger generation, difficulty adjusting to the retirement lifestyle, that sort of thing. My team and I have worked with Dave and Jan to get their financial plan and all their paperwork in order, but I believe they could really benefit from the kind of coaching you provide. May I introduce you?"

So it was that I found myself sitting at the Smith's kitchen table a week later. Dave and Jan, both in their early 60s, had jumped at the opportunity to meet, so eager were they to discuss their concerns and try to find a solution for effectively transferring their wealth and wisdom to the younger generations in their family. Dave, the patriarch, explained that he had just retired as the founding CEO of a wildly successful Fortune 50 company where he'd directed and mentored a group of extraordinary professionals for 30 years. Dave had reached the pinnacle in his field, amassing a fortune of over $50 million. Jan, the family matriarch, had dedicated her life to raising their three children and supporting her husband as he worked his way through his high-voltage career.

The couple's firstborn, Rob, and his wife, Meg, lived nearby. Rob was a periodontist who owned his own thriving practice. Meg had given up her career in advertising to become a stay-at-home mom for their energetic twin boys, Spence and Jack. Dave and Jan's eldest daughter, Suzy, and her husband, Mario, were successful artists and gallery owners living in Spain with their young daughter, Sofi. The Smith's remaining daughter, Amy, was twelve years younger than her siblings. An exceptionally bright young woman, Amy was studying for her MBA at an Ivy League college back east. Dave said that of all their children, Amy was the most financially savvy.

"That kid will run an empire someday, no doubt about it," Dave said with pride. "Don't get me wrong; it's not that Rob and Suzy aren't smart, because they are. It's just that Amy's got what it takes from a business and finance standpoint. So even though she's the baby of the family, she's going to be the one to settle our affairs when the time comes, and also run the charitable foundation we're planning to set up. For her sake we want to make sure that our wealth transfer plan is sound and as simple as it can be. Brian has helped us with that, and I think we're in pretty good shape. But we've got some family matters that could threaten the success of our plan. I guess that's why he recommended we meet with you."

Dave and Jan then spent the next three hours telling me all about the various challenges that had been keeping them up at night. First: neither of them were confident that Jan had the knowledge to manage their wealth should something happen to Dave.

"She's a smart gal, my wife," Dave said with a smile, "but I never gave her the chance to learn about our finances. I handled all that stuff myself because I like to do it, and also because I felt that she already had enough on her plate taking care of me and the house and the kids… especially our son, Rob. He was a handful, to put it mildly."

The Smith's explained that Rob had been extraordinarily rebellious during his teen years. Dave was so busy running his company that when he finally came home after a long day at the office, the last thing he wanted to do was confront a problematic kid. Consequently, Jan was forced to deal with the majority of Rob's challenges by herself; therefore, most of the discipline was dispensed by her. Jan didn't hold a grudge against Rob for giving them such a hard time when he was younger, but Dave did. He carried quite a bit of lingering resentment toward their son, as well as feelings of guilt for not being fully present to help Jan deal with him.

And that's why when Rob had announced that he wanted to become a periodontist, Dave made him finance his own schooling. He had two reasons for doing so. First of all, he didn't believe Rob would actually stick with dental school and he was not going to throw his money out the window on his son's latest whim. Second, he wanted to teach Rob a lesson about entitlement. The result was that Rob ended up with student loan debt of over $200,000. He also ended up with a lot of bitterness toward his dad. He couldn't understand why Dave—who was worth $50 million, remember—refused to help pay for his own son's education. He and Dave barely spoke for five years. But when Rob graduated with honors and Dave saw how dedicated his son was to his chosen profession, his heart softened. He offered to set Rob up with his own practice and give him whatever else he needed to be successful. Their relationship improved after that, but it was still not as close as any of them would have liked.

Neither were the Smith's satisfied with the quality of their relationship with Rob's wife, Meg, whom they described as "domineering" and "self-centered."

"You should see the way she pushes Rob around," Dave said with disgust. "He's about as hen-pecked as a guy can get. It's sickening. I can't stand knowing that our grandsons are being exposed to that every day. They're going to grow up thinking it's normal. And not only does Meg treat Rob like a servant, she acts as if Jan is invisible. There's no explanation for her behavior toward my wife. None whatsoever."

I doubt that, I thought. There is always an explanation if you dig deeply enough. I made a mental note to get to the bottom of Meg's problem with Jan.

Last but not least was the sad reality facing Suzy, their daughter living in Spain. Suzy's husband, Mario, had been battling cancer for three long years, and his prognosis was grim. Mario's health struggles had taken a terrible toll on Suzy, who had endured years of caring for him and their daughter Sofi while simultaneously running their Madrid art gallery alone. The entire family felt helpless and distraught over the unfolding tragedy in Suzy life. They were terribly concerned about the likelihood that she would soon become a widowed single mother, separated from her family by so many miles.

As Jan told me about their daughter's situation, her pain filled the room.

"This whole thing with Suzy and Mario has really knocked us to our knees," she said, dabbing her eyes with a tissue. "Yes, we have a lot of money. Yes, we can buy practically anything we want. But what's the point? All the money in the world won't save our daughter's husband. Our sweet little granddaughter's daddy is dying, for God's sake, and we can't fix it!"

"Our hearts are breaking over this," Dave sighed. "It's made us question our entire outlook on life, you know? And on top of everything else, I'm having a rough time adjusting to retirement. I guess that's why Brian suggested we talk to you. Are these the kinds of challenges you help people resolve?"

"I am so glad that you asked me that question," I replied.

I explained that I was not there to reinforce Brian's recommendations or give the Smith's a second opinion about their financial planning. I was not there to discuss insurance products and financial services. I was only there to help them and their kids better understand who they are; to help them uncover their deeper purpose and meaning as individuals, as a couple and as a family; to help them decide what kind of legacy they wanted to create and what significant roles they wanted to play as spouses, parents, grandparents, friends, neighbors and human beings; to help them create their customized family roadmap for

the way forward based on their unique journey and expressed in their own words, so that they would be remembered for what they stood for rather than how much money they had, for generations to come.

At that, Jan stood up.

"May I give you a hug?" she asked.

"Of course!" I said.

After our embrace, she turned to her husband.

"Dave, what do you think? May we work with Mayur? Please say yes!"

Dave nodded.

"Mayur, Jan and I have been married for 41 years and she has never asked me for anything until today," he said, "so I want to honor her request. When can we get started?"

"How about right now?" I replied.

The Smith's Discovery Process Begins

It didn't take long for me to determine that the Smith's were the typical affluent patriarch and matriarch: self-made, highly accomplished, extremely blunt and very trusting of those accepted into their inner circle. As life partners they were exceptionally trusting of one another too, and I immediately saw that Dave was an incredibly supportive family leader.

Still, they had some significant challenges to overcome, most notably:

- Incompatibility with the second generation, leading to multiple communication breakdowns and a lack of closeness.

- Uncertainty about Jan's ability to manage the family's financial affairs should the need arise.

- Inability to find the deeper meaning and purpose for creating a sustainable contribution going forward, especially for Dave as he adjusted to retirement.

Dave was just coming off a 30-year stint managing a group of fantastic professionals and generating tens of millions of dollars in income. It had been a heady existence and he had navigated it with great skill and enthusiasm. He'd truly loved his career. Now that it was over, he had no idea what to do with himself. He simply could not comprehend life after work. To fill the void, he began immersing himself into a variety of different hobbies and pursuits: hunting, fishing, dabbling in private equity investment, earning a pilot's license, becoming a certified SCUBA diver, mountaineering… you name it, Dave tried it. It was tough for his family to watch him bounce from one thing to another, searching and searching—for what, nobody knew—and then becoming increasingly frustrated when he didn't find what he was looking for. This wasn't the calm, cool and collected Dave they all knew and loved. Compound Dave's difficulties with the worry over Suzy and Mario and the lack of closeness with Rob and Meg, and the Smith's had a recipe for discontent.

To assess the extent of their upheaval, I had Dave and Jan fill out the Harmony Scorecard.

Completed Harmony Scorecard for Smith's

Initial ◆75

After 3 years ◆90

With a benchmark score of 75 percent, the Smith's were actually in fairly good shape as a group. All they needed was a tune up to reach the next level of family unity, and then a solid plan to sustain it. Toward that end, it was time to begin the Discovery process.

I explained to Dave and Jan that when I talk about Discovery, it is commonly misconstrued as an "interview" but in reality it is more of an "inner-view." Discovery empowers people to share what energizes them, what galvanizes them, what excites them, and what inspires them in addition to their corporate success.

We began by having Dave and Jan each fill out a Living Legacy Questionnaire, which revealed the following similarities in their childhoods: both were firstborns within families of cautious spenders. Both sets of parents instilled a strong work ethic and love of family, with honesty as a core value.

The questionnaire also highlighted differences in the way they were raised. Dave's mother controlled the finances in his childhood home. Money was a precious thing to Dave's mom. She insisted on buying only the best so it would last. Her greatest strength was her determination in the face of adversity, which made Dave mentally tough and likely contributed greatly to his success as an executive. Contrast that with Jan's upbringing. Dad controlled all the money in her childhood home, and his philosophy was that you must never buy anything you can't afford. When it came to Jan's mother, her greatest strength was her compassion. Consequently Jan grew to be an extraordinarily positive, financially modest and forgiving human being who was immensely grateful for the lessons imparted by both her parents.

Our Discovery then revealed that Dave and Jan shared one critical value in their adulthood—relationship with family—and they also shared a value that was least important to both of them: personal power. This would become important later in the process as we sought to bring all members of the family together and establish a direction they could all latch onto.

Next we inquired into the couple's key life insights. Dave's key insights were a penny saved is penny earned; money is precious so manage it prudently; leave a legacy of fairness and honesty; financial stewardship is a responsibility; and surround yourself with unequivocal love. Jan's life insights were never buy anything you cannot afford; be thankful for what you've got; love and respect one another; live life to the fullest; and money doesn't necessarily bring happiness. We then merged Dave and Jan's insights to form a combined "ethos of life" they could use to guide them and their kids forward:

- Financial stewardship is a responsibility

- Work is worship

- Leave a legacy of fairness and honesty

Next we asked Dave and Jan to name the one thing they were most certain about in life. Dave's response was that he was surrounded by love, and Jan's was that her family would always be her greatest support. We then asked them to tell us their biggest fear. Dave most feared a life-threatening event for one of his kids or grandkids. Jan cited being alone without Dave, or having one of her children pass before she did. We also inquired about what they thought was missing in their lives. Dave replied that nothing was missing (which was funny because he was certainly behaving like a man searching for something that was missing!). Jan wrote that she'd like to pursue her lifelong interest in writing without fear of failure. She'd always toyed with the idea of writing a novel but had lacked the confidence and courage to try.

The following segment of our inner view asked the Smith's to reflect on their feelings about one another. Their responses only confirmed what we'd already suspected: this was a couple with a great deal of love, respect and admiration for one another. They shared the same values and morals and looked forward to a long happy future together. But they both mentioned Jan's feelings of inadequacy when it came to financial matters, which was clearly a cause for concern.

When asked to describe their thoughts on their children, Dave and Jan expressed much love for and faith in each of their kids. They said they most valued Rob's easygoing attitude, Suzy's strength, and Amy's independence and business acumen. They also wrote of their joint concerns for each child. They wished Rob would assert himself more. They expressed their desire to take care of Suzy after Mario's passing. And for Amy, their biggest concerns were that she find a worthy life partner, and that the rest of the family would respect their choice to have her serve as executor of their estate and also head their family charitable foundation.

When it came to their feelings about their children-in-law, Dave and Jan wrote that they wished Suzy's husband Mario would be cured. But since that was an unlikely outcome, their concern was that his illness not threaten the stability of his family any more than it already had. As for Meg, the Smith's felt that she created unnecessary stress in the family. They wished she would focus more on Rob's needs and less on her own. Furthermore, they wished that her unexplained animosity toward Jan would be resolved.

We then asked the Smith's to give their thoughts about their grandchildren. Their joint wish was that all three grandkids would get top notch educations, and that they would grow up in loving environments with proper discipline. Naturally they were most concerned about little Sofi, who faced the prospect of losing her father at such a young age.

Next we asked Dave and Jan to comment on the universal principles holding their family together. It was no surprise that they both wrote that their family values, love and mutual respect for each other were responsible for keeping them close. Both also wrote that they appreciated how their kids shared a genuine love and concern for one another, and that they were all successful and productive.

When asked to name what they'd like to see happen in their family over the next three years, Dave wrote that he'd like to see Rob get his wife under control. Jan hoped that all three of their kids would have a better understanding of what she and their dad were trying to do for them through estate planning. And when asked to speculate on what the family would look like in ideal terms in 50 years, Dave wrote that the Smith's would go down in history as one of the century's greatest group of philanthropists. Jan's vision was more personal. She hoped that Rob and Suzy would be able to look back favorably on the paths they'd chosen, and that Amy would be a great support for her siblings in their golden years. When asked for their thoughts on leaving an inheritance for their kids, they responded that they wanted to be generous yet not leave so much that their heirs would become complacent about being productive and making a difference in the world.

We inquired about the Smith's current financial needs and charity. Both Dave and Jan indicated that they needed $600,000 annually to sustain their lifestyle, as well as $4 million in reserves to deal with the unexpected. They said they wanted to continue their charitable giving to Dave's alma mater, as well as supporting disaster relief, cancer research and other worthy causes.

Then we asked about Dave and Jan's health, their end-of-life plans and their spirituality. Both of them replied that they were in good physical condition.

They had all their final papers in order and they had discussed their last wishes between themselves and also with each of their children. They felt totally at ease and were confident that the family was prepared to deal with all aspects of their passing when the time came. The Smith's were also in agreement on their spirituality. Both Dave and Jan wrote that although they were not especially religious, their spiritual beliefs gave them strength. They said they would like to leave a spiritual legacy in the form of family values, tradition and honesty.

Our line of questioning then turned to Dave a`nd Jan's reflections on their careers. When asked to name his life's work, Dave replied, "I was a builder. I built things for the betterment of humanity and achieved the impossible." He said his greatest concern for his wealth was that too much of it would go to the government and be wasted. When asked to describe her life's work, Jan replied, "I was the best mother, wife and friend that I could be." Her biggest concern about their wealth was being able to construct a great inheritance plan.

And lastly, we asked Dave and Jan to think about the purpose of their lives. Dave replied that he was a dedicated family man, husband and father as well as a great leader, motivator and strategic thinker. He was proud of having mentored so many of his colleagues. He looked forward to channeling his energy toward new tasks and activities, especially creating a foundation to do good works. With unlimited resources, he wanted to travel more with his family. If there were a plaque in his honor, he would like it to read, "Dave Smith:

A Man of Infinite Integrity Who Was Respected By All Who Crossed His Path."

When asked to reflect on the purpose of her life, Jan replied that above all else she had tried to be the kind of wife and mom that her family could look up to. Supporting her family was her greatest achievement. At this point in her life, she was energized by the prospect of pursuing her dream of becoming a novelist.

She hoped to begin attending writer's conferences, taking some creative writing classes and spending more time with her kids and grandkids. If there were a plaque left in her honor, she would like it to read, "Jan Smith: A Loving Mother, Wife and Grandmother Who Will Live On In The Memories Of Those She Cherished."

Now that we had an idea of Dave and Jan's strengths, concerns and opportunities for growth, it was time to bring their kids into the mix. The first thing I wanted to do was get at the source of the tension between Jan and their daughter-in-law, Meg. I asked if I might give Meg a call.

"Sure, why not?" Dave said, as Jan nodded her approval. "Frankly, I can't wait to hear what she has to say. Let me get her on the phone for you."

Chapter 9:

Opening Hearts and Expanding Minds

Committed elders have the power to transform their entire family.

After Dave explained to Meg who I was and gave her a general overview of my role as their family's wealth coach, he asked her if she'd be willing to chat with me for a few minutes. She agreed.

As I introduced myself, I could tell from the hesitancy in Meg's voice that she was a little intimidated and wary of what was to come. I did my best to ease her into the honest conversation I wanted us to have about her behavior toward Jan. I explained that my job was to guide families like theirs through a process of establishing a unified path into the future; to strengthen their ties to one another across the generations and to help them achieve clarity about how they might use their family's

I assured her that as the wife of Dave and Jan's only son and the mother of two of their three grandkids, she would play a starring role in establishing and furthering the Smith Family legacy. I told her that her in-laws wished to be closer to her and I wanted to help make that happen. Then I asked Meg to tell me about herself. Where did she grow up? Who were her parents? What was her life like before she met Rob?

Within 15 minutes, I had solved the mystery of why Meg had been treating Jan with such disdain. It turned out that Meg's mother and father had divorced with she was in elementary school, and her mother quickly married another man. Meg's mom devoted all her time and attention to her new relationship, leaving Meg to fend for herself and take care of her younger sibling.

"I didn't have much of a childhood because of that," Meg said. "I felt totally abandoned by our mom. She wasn't 'there' for us, you know what I mean? It hurt so much. So I distanced myself from her emotionally and then physically. I moved out of her house as soon as I graduated from high school and that was the end of that. I still don't trust her to this day. She was a terrible mother."

I then asked Meg the million dollar question: Could it be that she was bundling her pent-up frustration with her mother and aiming it at Jan instead? Put another way, was it possible that all her unresolved pain and distrust of her mother might be adversely affecting her relationship with her mother-in-law?

There was silence on the other end of the line for a few seconds, followed by sniffles and a muffled reply: "That's a possibility, I suppose."

"That would be understandable, after all you've been through," I replied. "But let me ask you this, Meg, as the mother of two little boys: would you like your children or your children's future spouses to treat you the way you've treated Jan?"

Now Meg's sniffles became sobs.

"No, of course not!" she cried.

"So what shall we do about this?" I asked.

"Mayur, please put Jan on the phone," Meg replied.

What followed was an amazing healing moment for the Smith family. Meg assured Jan that she'd done nothing to deserve the terrible treatment Meg had given her. She apologized profusely for hurting her (and by extension, Dave) and she begged for their forgiveness.

Jan's compassion for her daughter-in-law was evident as she accepted her apology and promised to be there for her every single day for the rest of her life.

"You can count on me, Meg," Jan said. "This momma will not let you down."

A Family Retreat

Before I left the Smith's home that first day, I asked them to reach out to their kids and explain to them what we were doing, and also to tell them to expect to hear from me within a week. I was going to have each of them to fill out a Second Generation Questionnaire in advance of the family retreat we were planning for the following month. Time was of the essence for two reasons. First, Mario's health was deteriorating rapidly; and second, Dave and Jan wanted to fast-track the process for the simple reason that they were excited about it.

Communicating with the Smith's children and their spouses was a pleasure. They were taking the process very seriously and were eager to see it unfold. I explained that the questionnaires I'd sent were designed to help them crystallize their beliefs and attitudes about wealth, family and values. Through these thought-provoking questions, they would be stimulated to search for the honest answers lying deep within their hearts, minds and souls. These questions would not necessarily be easy ones, but there were no wrong answers.

All five kids—Rob, Meg, Suzy, Mario and Amy—were quick to fill out and return their questionnaires, which we used to create "Reflections of Life" for each of them and a "Values Matrix" for their entire family in anticipation of the upcoming retreat, which would be held a resort spa near the Smith's home. In the weeks leading up to the retreat, Rob rearranged his patient schedule, Meg secured onsite childcare for the boys, and Amy made flight reservations. Unfortunately Mario was unable to travel, so he and Suzy would be attending the day-long meeting via the internet.

The agenda for the retreat was simple. First we'd hold a 90-minute group meeting, and afterward I'd meet with every couple and Amy separately for a little over an hour each.

On the day of the retreat I kicked things off by giving the kids some background on why the meeting was taking place, as well as an explanation of what we hoped would come of it.

"Let me start by asking you some questions," I said to the group. "Do you change the mattress on your bed every day? Probably not. How about your toothbrush… did you throw out the one you used yesterday and reach for a fresh one this morning? No? What about the shower head in your bathroom; did you install a new one today? I doubt it. Then why are you and the other members of your family changing your thoughts and direction every day? In order to create the most impact, it is critical to establish a direction and then stick to it. You must understand and identify who you are, why you are here, what matters most to you and what you would like to establish as a living legacy. This understanding must happen on two levels: as individuals and as a family. And that's the reason for this retreat."

Then I presented Dave and Jan's Reflections of Life and Ethos of Life, which were the results of their Legacy Questionnaires. The kids were quite moved by this. Up to then they'd never really had enough information to connect the dots and understand the underlying reasons for their parents' personal and professional values, actions and beliefs. Rob was especially touched by Dave's reflection of working on a farm for less than minimum wage when he was young. He was also surprised by his father's frank admission that he sometimes treated others with condescension—a behavior he regretted and was trying hard to change.

Next I unveiled the Smith Family Values Matrix, which merged the results of everyone's questionnaires into the one easy-to-digest graphic. The Values Matrix highlights the mutually complimentary contributions of each family member and illustrates how each person's passion and gifts can be used to benefit all the others.

Smith Family Values Matrix

Values Matrix

Dave	Jane	Rob	Suzy
Honesty	Honesty	Making a difference	Relationship with family
Integrity	Kindness	accomplishments	Connecting
Spirituality	Spirituality	Relationship with family	Passion
bonding	Relation with family	trust	trust
commitment	Physical well being	Spirituality	Integrity

What we had before us was a visual illustration of each person's values as they related to the dynamics of the family. This allowed us to link the Smith family members in a way that had never been done before. For example, Dave shared the value of Making a Difference with his daughter, Suzy. Several family members shared the value of Happiness, and most of them cited Physical Health as a value worth nurturing. The Smith's had a good time studying the matrix and figuring out which values they had in common with whom.

I recall two particular AHA! moments as we went through this exercise with the Smith family. First was when Jan and Meg realized that they shared the value of Relationship with Family. This caused them to pause and reaffirm their commitment to improving their relationship for the benefit of the entire family. It was a happy and tearful moment for all of them.

The second AHA! moment was between Dave and Rob. Dave was delighted to learn that he and his son shared the value of Integrity, and he was more than a little surprised to see how much Rob valued Education and Accomplishments and Results. Dave asked Rob if there was a particular type of learning he was interested in pursuing, and Rob replied that he'd like to know more about business and management because he was thinking of expanding his practice and would need to upgrade his knowledge and skill set to be successful.

"Actually, maybe you could tutor me on that, Dad," Rob said. "Nobody knows that stuff better than you."

Again, more happy tears were shed.

The effect of this exercise was to break the traditional patriarch/matriarch-child relationship. In its place was now a circle of excellence in which every member of the family understood their contribution to the well-being of everybody else. It was an awesome epiphany for the Smith's. They were no longer focused on biases, assumptions, or opinions about one another. They had before them a foundation upon which they could proactively build a living legacy; a guiding light they could use to illuminate the way to the highest level of trust, respect and honor in their family.

With that in mind, I guided them as they brainstormed to create a family motto. They settled on "ONE FOR ALL, ALL FOR ONE." In light of this new motto, Mario was assured that he was not alone and that everyone in the family was on his side to meet his personal, emotional and spiritual needs. In fact, Dave and Jan offered to travel to Madrid immediately with the intention of renting a nearby flat for at least two months, to help out in any way they could. Their offer was quickly and gratefully accepted by Suzy and Mario.

Dave and Jan then asked me to educate all the children regarding the proposed strategies we'd developed to achieve the following:

1. Shrink the taxable estate and reduce future estate tax liability from 55 percent to 25 percent

2. Protect assets from creditors.

3. Provide income for life for Dave and Jan.

4. Allow Dave and Jan to keep control of investable assets for the foreseeable future.

5. Freeze assets at a discounted value for the rest of Dave's and Jan's lives.

6. Provide a loan to the proposed grantor trust at a very attractive rate.

7. Create flexibility in the grantor trust so that income and assets could be used for funding health, education, maintenance and support for children and grandchildren; as well as access to capital for specific life events like home purchases, down payments for businesses, expanding Rob's practice and co-investment opportunities.

Finally, we set up a communication schedule to ensure that there would be plenty of touchpoints between the family members going forward. Jan and Meg would get together for an afternoon out a minimum of once per month, and every kid would check in with their parents and each other on a weekly basis. Dave would also begin mentoring and spending more time with Rob. For example, the men would take three father-son trips per year for hunting and fly fishing—activities both enjoyed. The goal was to provide opportunities for Dave to pass on his wealth of wisdom to his son, thereby grooming Rob for his future role as the family patriarch. The entire family would meet virtually every quarter, and in person annually.

Next came the individual meetings. I started with Rob and Meg, who said that the discussion about the Values Matrix had been a genuine eye-opener for them. Meg said she realized that she had been taking far too many things for granted, and she looked forward to becoming a more active and positive part of the Smith family. Rob disclosed that he wished he were a skilled visionary like his dad, and I assured him that he had the ability to achieve that goal. Spending time with Dave, as I'd recommended, would go a long way toward getting him there. Rob wholeheartedly agreed. I asked him to put together a three-year professional road map describing the ways he might grow, and also sketch out the potential impact of creating a profit center approach with his business rather than the gross revenue approach he was currently taking. He promised to do so immediately and to share it with me and his dad so we could offer input.

I also suggested that he and Meg sit down together to prioritize each of their life goals and dreams, and send that to me too. And since Meg paid the household bills each month, I asked her to forward her expense spreadsheet right away so I could begin to help them balance their budget. I requested that they send all their information to me within six weeks so I could have time to analyze it all before our next quarterly meeting. Accountability is key!

Then it was Amy's turn to meet. We discussed her unique journey regarding her education, and we also talked about a young man she'd been dating. Dylan was a Judge Advocate General in the Air Force. Amy was beginning to think he might be "the one." Dylan was obligated to serve for several more years, and Amy shared that she was willing to adjust her plans to coincide with his assignments, wherever that might lead her. With Happiness as one of her core values, this was no surprise. I recommended that she speak to her father about this and capture the essence of their communications in a journal which she would share with me monthly. By talking to Dave, Amy would also be learning more about financial literacy and fiscal governance in preparation for her managing the family foundation and also her personal wealth. I asked her to email me her bank, IRA and credit card statements so I could create her income and expense analysis and balance sheet. I reminded her that when Dave and Jan pass away, she and her siblings were likely to inherit in excess of $20 million, so it was necessary for her to develop the skills and emotional readiness to manage this wealth over the next three to five years.

I also reminded her to communicate once a week with Suzy and continue to offer her support, and to also communicate with Rob to strengthen their relationship. We discussed Amy's intention to make philanthropic contributions of her time and talents. I suggested that she, Suzy and Mario put their heads together and identify different causes and organizations that could become partners to help the family pursue their charitable endeavors. I also recommended that she spend time with Dylan and his parents at least once per quarter.

Lastly, I went online to meet with Suzy and Mario. We started off with the happy fact that they would soon be closing on a new house in Madrid. They needed $75,000 to fix up the place, so I offered to talk to Dave and create a way to pay for that. We then discussed Mario's declining health. He said he was frustrated, anguished and emotionally down because he'd tried every medical treatment offered to him as well as every holistic, alternate and Ayurvedic therapy, but there had been no major change in his health. I gave him insight on breathing exercises and meditation and offered to connect him with a group of oncologists I know. I asked him to send all his medical reports so I could forward them to the physicians. I also promised to put him in touch with a spiritual counselor who would guide him over the coming weeks.

Next, we talked about the Values Matrix. I noted that Mario's values of Happiness and Emotional Health were suffering now, so I emphasized the need for him to shift his mental paradigm from being disheartened to being creative through his art. Mario was a gifted sculptor but he had essentially stopped working over the past year as he'd become increasingly ill and dispirited. I encouraged him to begin anew… but this time not with the goal of creating something for their gallery. This time I wanted him to create a work of art especially for his daughter, Sofi—to put all the love, spirit and hope he had into that sculpture. We set a deadline of one month for the project to be completed. I also recommended that he spend quality time with Sofi and Suzy, setting an intention each day to be happy by making them happy.

I then turned to Suzy. She had clearly done an amazing job balancing her professional life, parental responsibilities and companionship for Mario, who was deeply appreciative and grateful for that. For additional support, I recommended that they make an effort to be emotionally engaged with Dave and Jan as well as Mario's parents during this difficult time. Lastly, I requested that Suzy continue to budget and trail their expenses, and also send their financial paperwork for my review.

Meeting Adjourned… For Now

After the individual meetings were finished, I brought everyone back together again—including Suzy and Mario via the internet—for a few closing thoughts before they went their separate ways. Here is what I told them…

Always remember that the more you focus your attention on something, the more it becomes a part of your life. If you decide to focus on your weaknesses, deficits and fears, you will get MORE weakness, MORE deficits and MORE fear.

On the other hand, when you choose to focus your attention on your strengths, abundance and courage, you will get MORE strength, MORE abundance and MORE courage.

You cannot turn a weakness into a strength.

Regardless of the level of dysfunction you are facing as individuals and as a family, it's safe to say that what you need most is clarity. Smith Family, you now have more clarity than you had when you came into this meeting. And now that you have this level of clarity, you are more open and receptive to new ways of thinking. You will be capable of mentoring others with empathy and complete humility. Negative feelings of attachment will be replaced by healthy feelings of detachment. You will begin giving without any expectation of a return—which is the only way to truly give.

Once your inner core is filled with this kind of detachment, you are no longer entitlement-driven. You no longer feel disappointed by unmet expectations. You no longer will feel that other people are out to hurt you. You can begin feeling grateful for others being part of your life, for giving you wisdom and for showing you the path of enlightenment. You will radiate the knowledge that you came into this lifetime alone as a soul and you shall leave this lifetime alone as a soul. You will seek to be remembered

That is what the sustainability of wisdom, values, business savvy and family best practices is all about. Very few families get to bottom of what is preventing them from taking these things to the next level, but you are on your way. You are on the right road now, as individuals and as a family.

And so until we meet again, I urge you to continue down this road with grateful and optimistic hearts. Although this journey is well worth taking, it is not without its challenges. Please remember that I am always here to guide you and to facilitate your empowerment. I have no ownership in your progress. I am merely a quiet performer in the background, helping you do what you need to do in order to share and grow.

With that, the group disbursed with an extremely high energy level, full of enthusiasm, emotional engagement, and most of all, hope.

Chapter 10:

Smith Family Update

> *Transferring wealth and wisdom is a way of life.*

Five years have passed since that first family retreat, and I'm pleased to report that the Smith's have prospered. Dave, the extraordinary founding CEO of a large multi-national company, has turned out to be as terrific a leader in retirement as he was in his professional career. In addition to his impressive personal wealth, he has gone on to amass fantastic emotional and spiritual wealth with the same level of commitment he gave to the first 35 years of his corporate life. He is now much less scattered and much more liberated. He is making efforts to simplify his life, including exiting the majority of the private equities he'd invested in initially. He says he'd rather devote his time to his family and his expertise to making a difference through his philanthropic efforts, all of which perfectly dovetail with his values now.

Jan reached higher and farther than she would have allowed herself to imagine five years ago. Rather than attending a few writer's workshops as she had planned, she decided to earn a Master of Fine Arts degree in creative writing. She completed her first novel last year and is looking for a literary agent to represent her as she tries to get a book deal from a major publisher. Jan, who was admittedly financially naïve five years ago, is today extremely confident in her ability to manage their wealth should the need arise because she took advantage of the many learning opportunities we presented to her. She's now on top of everything when it comes to their finances.

Rob expanded his practice with financial help from Dave and Jan. The practice is now a thriving high-profile business in their community. Rob and Dave have continued their tradition of three father/son trips each year, including one annual trip that includes Rob's twin boys. Meg and Jan are closer than ever. They're currently having a great time redecorating the condo that Dave and Jan helped them purchase.

Amy finished her MBA and is working for a venture capital firm in addition to managing the family foundation. She and Dylan were married and were recently blessed with a beautiful baby daughter. Dylan, inspired by wife's and father-in-law's business success, applied to an Ivy League MBA program in anticipation of his upcoming discharge from the military. He and Amy enjoy spending weekends at the seaside condo Dave and Jan helped them buy.

And then there's Suzy. Sadly, Mario passed away a year after that first family retreat. It was a devastating blow for the whole family, but they took comfort in knowing that Mario's final year was one of great closeness, sharing and creativity. Not only did he make that special sculpture for Sofi, he also made one for Dave and Jan, who had followed through on their pledge to spend two months in Madrid to be there for him and Suzy in their moment of need. The sculpture now occupies a treasured spot in Dave and

Jan's family room and in their hearts. A couple of years after Mario's passing, Suzy met and married Alán, a kind, brilliant physician who has become a valued member of the family and a wonderful father for Sofi.

At our last family retreat, we had the entire Smith family fill out a new Harmony Scorecard. What a revelation! Their score had increased from 75 percent to an amazing 90 percent family harmony. Yet they are not satisfied to rest on their laurels. They intend to reach even higher by continually refining their family governance roadmap for passing on their wealth and wisdom to the third generation and beyond.

PART 4:
THE CORDERO'S

A Family That Doesn't Know What They Don't Know

Chapter 11:

Meet the Cordero's

> *You come into the world ignorant and you leave the world*
> *enlightened to the extent of your own commitment,*
> *courage and communication.*
> *This is what makes life worth living.*

Within the first few minutes of meeting Diego and Maria
Cordero, I realized two important facts about them. First, these
people had started at less-than-zero and had gone on to create
something truly impressive—a collection of hotels worth over
$100 million. Second, the dysfunction in their family threatened to
destroy everything they'd worked so hard to build.

The Cordero's were in their late 60s when we met three years
ago at the urging of their corporate attorney. Diego explained that
he and his wife had immigrated to the United States from their
rural South American village when they were in their early 20s,
arriving with nothing but the clothes on their backs, a strong work
ethic, and a lot of hope for a brighter future. They settled in South
Florida.

"Tourism was booming in the region in those days," Diego said,
"so there was plenty of work in hospitality. Both of us found jobs
in hotels right away. I worked in landscaping and maintenance,
and Maria in housekeeping. Our son, Pedro, was born a few years
after we arrived in America."

Diego explained that Pedro's birth only strengthened his and
Maria's resolve to succeed in their adopted country. They were
determined to give their little boy all the opportunities and
material things they'd lacked as children growing up in

poverty-stricken farm families. Although the Cordero's never hesitated to spend money buying Pedro the latest toys and taking him and his friends on fun outings, they were frugal when it came to spending on themselves. Instead they scrimped and saved for their dream of buying their own little hotel someday.

To further that goal, Diego and Maria took English classes at a neighborhood school, earned U.S. citizenship, and learned everything they could about the hospitality industry through on-the-job training. They were both promoted in their jobs multiple times, eventually leading them into management roles with increased responsibility and higher earnings. A successful entrepreneur took the couple under his wing and mentored them, introducing them to some of the area's most prosperous leaders in business, hospitality and real estate.

Fast forward 40 years and the Cordero's had achieved their business goal… and then some. Their empire, which started with one humble fixer-upper, eventually grew to include multiple boutique hotels. Their business model was to purchase rundown properties in up-and-coming tourist areas, renovate them, use their vast experience to get them operating at peak performance, and sell them for a hefty profit. They also retained ownership of a few small beachfront hotels simply for the joy of running them.

With an eye toward passing on their company to Pedro someday, Diego and Maria urged their son to apply to one of the nation's top business administration programs. He was accepted. Although his grades were less than stellar, he stuck with the program and earned his degree. Pedro met his future wife, Julia, in college. The young couple married immediately after graduation, and Pedro went to work in his parents' business. He and Julia soon had two children, Angelica and Andres, who were now in their early 20s.

Diego and Maria explained that they had essentially handed over the day-to-day operations of the business to their son seven years prior. The original idea was to stay close to Pedro in the beginning but to gradually ease themselves out of the company as he demonstrated proficiency in running and developing the business.

"Pedro told us all along that taking over the company was what he wanted to do," Maria said. "We set him up to succeed... or so we thought."

"Yes, Pedro has been a huge disappointment when it comes to managing operations and development," Diego said. "He spent 45-years watching me build and run this business but he acts like he just walked through the door yesterday. It's one stupid mistake after another. He never learns! And when I try to guide him, he blows up and tells me to get off his back. He says I don't trust his judgment. Well, he's right. I don't."

As a result, Diego and his heir apparent had suffered disconnect and disengagement seven times in seven years, always letting their emotions drive their behavior rather than thinking rationally. The pattern was that Diego would get confused about a business decision Pedro had made. The two would argue about it and then clear things up (but only superficially; symptomatically). It wouldn't be long before Diego became confrontational again, spurring yet another argument with Pedro followed by a cursory reconciliation. Consequently the Cordero's business and family lives were utter chaos. The ongoing conflict had affected Maria's health to the extent that she was clinically depressed, some days finding it impossible to leave her bedroom. We needed to get to the bottom of this immediately.

The Cordero's Discovery Process Begins

Before we could begin to bring clarity to the Cordero's, we first had to identify their most pressing issues. There were many challenges to choose from, but I decided to focus on addressing these three:

- The entitlement-driven attitude of the second generation.
- A victim mentality shared by all members of the family.
- Lack of contentment.

Since Maria was so fragile, we had her and Diego work together to complete a Harmony Scorecard and Legacy Questionnaire rather than having them do the exercises separately. Their Harmony Scorecard came out with the lowest result my team and I have ever seen:

Completed Harmony Scorecard for CORDERO'S

Initial ◆ **22**

After 3 years ◆ **75**

With a benchmark score of only 22 percent family harmony, it was clear that the Cordero's had a lot of work ahead of them. I reminded them that they had started from the bottom and risen to the top before, and they could do it again. I would be by their side every step of the way.

I explained to Diego and Maria that our strategy for increasing family harmony and laying the groundwork for an effective succession has five aspects:

1. Discover and pass on the patriarch/matriarch's values, ethos and insights.

2. Increase financial literacy and wealth education across the generations.

3. Strengthen communication through family meetings.

4. Define and implement a plan for values-based family philanthropy.

5. Develop effective family governance through retreats, mediation, and family council.

The first step on their path to healing was filling out the Living Legacy Questionnaire. From it we learned that Diego and Maria were both middle-born children from large farm families that struggled to afford even the basic necessities of life. Their families were, however, very close and caring. For them, sharing and hard work were valued above all else. The one event that had the greatest positive impact on both of the Cordero's was coming to the United States together as young adults. The event that had had the most adverse impact on them was the negative cash flow of $1 million they'd suffered at their largest property in the aftermath of the 9/11 terrorist attacks. Had they not had sufficient savings and positive cash flow elsewhere, they would have gone out of business. They were terribly afraid of something like that happening again, either because of circumstances beyond their control or because of Pedro's perceived bad decision-making.

Diego and Maria stated that they shared the same set of values: always remembering their humble beginnings, a strong work ethic, and spirituality. Among their greatest accomplishments were the trust they'd built among their family members, business associates, community and employees; as well as the financial stability they'd achieved.

When it came to their feelings about their son, Diego and Maria said they loved Pedro with all their hearts. They considered him to be humble, honest, intelligent, and compassionate toward others. They still had a great deal of hope for his future even though they worried about his current ability to manage his money and the business. They loved their daughter-in-law, Julia, but their relationships with her and the grandkids, Angelica and Andres, were not as close as they would have liked because of the constant conflict over the business. They feared that their grandchildren might become trapped by materialism, and that they might forget their South American heritage and spirituality. They also worried that Pedro and Julia might not manage their wealth properly, thereby threatening Angelica and Andres' inheritance. The Cordero's wrote that they wished Pedro and Julia would learn to live a simpler lifestyle, and that Julia would "help make a better businessman out of our son." Diego and Maria also wished that the younger generations in their family had more respect for the skills and abilities their patriarch and matriarch had developed. One bright spot in their lives: they cherished their family's unique sense of humor.

"We've always been able to laugh together," Maria said. "But we're not laughing as much as we used to. All we do is worry about when the next fight is going to come."

The questionnaire then asked the Cordero's to name three aspects of their family life that they thought were most urgently in need of improvement. They cited openness to change, communication between different generations and effective communication between all generations. When asked for their greatest certainties in life, *they said trust in God, love for others and compassion for the needy. Their greatest fear: effectively passing and maintaining wealth from the first generation to the second to the third.*

Next we asked the Cordero's to give us their greatest insights of life. They responded: by working hard, we have pushed *ourselves to success; we never forget our humble beginnings; and we keep life simple and spiritual.* When asked how they would like to be remembered should there be a plaque in their honor, they responded, "The Cordero's: Humble, Kind, Family-Focused People."

At this point we had enough information about Diego and Maria's values to create an "ethos of life" they could use to guide their family forward:

- **Success is gained by hard work**
- **Be good to others**
- **Responsibility is always with me**

The time h ad come to share this information with the younger generations of the Cordero family. We called a family meeting between Diego, Maria, Pedro and Julia. This is what I told them…

Chapter 12:

Realigning Focus

> ## This isn't about what you have. It's about what you do with what you have.

In the conventional wisdom, children learn everything they need to know from their elders. They learn by observing what the older ones do, how they teach, the values they share and what the family environment gave them as a gift. When children become adults they apply everything they learned, in essence passing on their elders' values, wisdom, and wealth—their legacy—to the world. Some families are more effective at this transfer process than others. The big difference in terms of effectiveness seems to be how skilled the family is at filling the gaps: gaps in communication, in expectation management and in mindset.

If the patriarch/matriarch's mindset is an unwillingness to relinquish control and have empathy for the younger ones, then the transfer process will not be as effective as it could be. When the elders are hypercritical, the younger ones eventually become indifferent, causing the elders to become vicious as they seek to protect what they have built. This tug-of-war eventually becomes a lose-lose situation for everyone involved. No progress can be made; no meaningful legacy transfer can take place.

The same is true if the mindset of the younger generation is one of entitlement. In this case there is a lack of cooperation because they are not thinking of themselves as an important part of a unique circle trying to create a better world. Their obstruction leads to resentment, confrontation, discomfort, disillusionment, disappointment and anxiety. There is no team spirit; no shared vision, mission or purpose between the generations. The lack of shared vision, mission and purpose leads to an attitude of "What's in it for me? Why are you making me suffer when you have so much?" rather than "What can we do together to make a difference?"

An absence of shared vision, mission and purpose is a major threat to your family. It is like a landmine you are all being forced to walk over every day—a landmine that can be extremely destructive to your family's wealth, longevity and harmony, as one notorious American family learned the hard way.

The Vanderbilt's: A Cautionary Tale

In the early 1800s, a young man named "Commodore" Vanderbilt borrowed $100 from his mom and started a ferry business on New York's Staten Island. Commodore's enterprise eventually grew to include steamboats and ultimately led him to build a booming nationwide railroad company that for a time controlled all the rail traffic in and out of New York City. When Commodore Vanderbilt died in the late 1870s, he was worth $100 million—more than was contained in the entire U.S. Treasury.

Commodore's son, Billy, took over the railway business and expanded it. When he passed away 15 years later, the Vanderbilt fortune was worth twice what it was when he inherited it. Despite Commodore's wish that the family's remaining shares of the company be passed on to only one person for the sake of continuity, Billy split them between his two sons.

By then the Vanderbilt's had accumulated all of the material perks of being ultra-affluent during the Gilded Age: multiple mansions, luxurious yachts, limousines, a magnificent art collection, an impressive array of jewels, thoroughbred horses… you name it, the Vanderbilt's had it. They were also notable philanthropists, creating and endowing Vanderbilt University and giving generously to various other entities and causes.

But the world was changing. Rail transport was gradually being replaced by trucks, barges and planes. So while the Vanderbilt's were preoccupied with their extravagant spending and unchecked giving, their business—and their fortune—began slipping away. Their income was falling, but their spending was not.

Can you guess where we're headed here?

Today there is not a single millionaire left among the Vanderbilt's, because some people within the third and subsequent generations simply couldn't handle the abundance of wealth that had been bestowed upon them. They became misdirected in their giving. Some of them got corrupt hearts. The entire family fell apart because of greed, because of jealousy, because of mutual confrontation, and because of their entitlement attitude. Consequently, the lifetime work of Commodore Vanderbilt, the family patriarch, ended in bankruptcy. The Vanderbilt's are indeed a cautionary tale for all affluent families.

Contrast the Vanderbilt saga with that of another wealthy American family: the Rockefeller's. John D. Rockefeller Sr., co-founder of Standard Oil in the 1870s, lived by a basic principle he'd adopted during his early years, which was keep the family together. Having meals with his wife and four kids, talking about their day, worshiping together, traveling together along the road of business and life with no expectations beyond simply sharing the journey as a family… this was the Rockefeller way.

The result was that over time and across generations the Rockefeller's learned from the values and ethos of the family patriarch. In the 1950s they began holding family meetings for that sole purpose. Their shared life experience created wonderful insights for the younger ones. One of them became a senator, another made the decision to become a philanthropist. Several of them continued the business journey started by John Sr. and today, well over 100 Rockefeller's are multi-millionaires. To this day they still make it a point to have a family meeting at least twice a year.

The Rockefeller's have rallied around the goal of empowerment to affect a positive change in the community they are part of and the industries they want to transform. The Rockefeller Foundation is making mainstream impact with over six billion dollars in their endowed funds. This has become the most respected nonprofit in the world, bar none. They've created opportunities for others not by donating but by giving grants and creating a shared accountability.

> *All of us owe our gratitude to the Rockefeller's-especially to the patriarch who laid the foundation of wealth and wisdom necessary to sustain it for generations.*

For example, the family has given millions in grants to the Rockefeller lab at Memorial Sloan Kettering Hospital, which saves lives through cancer research. Memorial Sloan Kettering is now the world's most perennial and respected institute in cancer breakthroughs. Then there's Rockefeller University, which has transformed the futures of hundreds of thousands of people.

The Pew Charitable Trusts, the Bill and Melinda Gates Foundation and the Rockefeller Foundation are considered to be benchmarks for how philanthropy should be done. Did the Rockefeller's have any proficiency in doing this when they first started? Absolutely not. They learned from their life experience. They learned from sharing with others, understanding what is important to the younger generations, and empowering them to follow their passion. You can do the same. And when you do, you will not only help your community and the world, but you will also strengthen your family. You will pass on not only your wealth but also your values, for decades to come. You will provide a steady compass your descendants can use to guide them forward. When you share as a family, you grow as a family.

And so now I ask you, which path do you want to follow: the path of the Vanderbilt's or the Rockefeller's? The choice truly is yours to make. I'm going to assume you'd rather move into the future like the Rockefeller's. But before you begin, you must understand three key concepts: detachment, entitlement and contentment.

Detachment, Entitlement and Contentment

Detachment is the ultimate liberation in life. As a legendary mentor, world-class CEO, accomplished entrepreneur, life-saving doctor, amazing family leader, the wealthiest person in your community—whatever your situation may be—everyone has put you up on a very tall pedestal. You have been showered with glowing accolades for so long, you may have begun to believe your own press. You have become attached to the image of your adjectives rather than maintaining your inner core and following what it tells you to do.

But here's the truth:

1. **When you are attached to that image of yourself, you are limited.**

2. **When you are attached to outcomes, you are vulnerable.**

3. **When you are attached to the actions of other people, you are chained.**

Why is this the truth? Because nobody, nobody—and I repeat a third time—nobody, is yours.

All of us operate under the illusion that our families love us, our clients love us, the community loves us selflessly, but in reality, As human beings we have conditional relationships with one another for a certain period of time, and that's that. Only exception are enlightened human beings.

You came into this world alone (unless you were a twin, and even then you were separated by a minute!) and you will pass from this world alone. But the most amazing part of the life journey is that you will never, ever, travel alone. You travel with other people.

As a member of the first generation in your twilight years, if you can empower yourself to detach from every single emotional and professional relationship you have built and follow your passion for the rest of your life, you will enjoy a state of bliss and freedom; of being in paradise.

You will be able to communicate your message without speaking a word.

You will be able to perpetuate your legacy. That is detachment.

And then there is entitlement. Most people in the world remain works-in-progress because they always revert to their entitlement-driven expectations. See if any of these statements sound familiar to you:

- "As the patriarch, I did EVERYTHING to create prosperity in this family. But when I try to help the younger ones and give them advice, they treat me like I'm a nuisance. Why won't anyone listen to me now?"

- "As the matriarch, I did EVERYTHING to keep my family together and strong. Now that I'm older, my kids and grandkids are all moving away. Sometimes they don't even return my calls. Why aren't they supporting me? It's my turn!"

- "I have done so much for this community, but what do I get in return? Nothing! Why is everyone so ungrateful and disrespectful? Why don't they recognize all I've done?"

• "My wife told me not to be so generous, but I didn't listen. Now look at what I am going through! My daughter-in-law is treating me like dirt. My son believes he's entitled to all the money. My granddaughter, I love her from the bottom of my heart and they are not letting me play with her. My daughter went through a bitter divorce because her husband was the greediest SOB, and she lost everything I gave her. Why is our family such a mess?

Look around you. So many people are in so much pain. They are spinning and spinning in the midst of chaos, feeling like victims… always feeling that everybody has taken advantage of them, taken advantage of their money, taken advantage of their generosity.

When you have chaos, confusion accelerates.

When confusion accelerates, your vision becomes blurred.

When your vision becomes blurred you seek instant gratification because you believe you are entitled to it. And you are never happy.

That is the danger of entitlement.

The third key concept to remember if you want to live like a Rockefeller is contentment. Let's say you usually eat three square meals a day. This makes you content; you are happy that your need for food is being met.

But what if you haven't yet nurtured a deep commitment to being content in your life?

One day you may be eating delicious food from a paper plate and you look up to find somebody else eating delicious food from a silver platter. And what happens? You suddenly forget about the quality of the food you are eating. You forget about the fact that your nutritional needs are met on a daily basis, and you think, "Oh, my God! Why am I not fortunate enough to eat from the silver platter too? It's not fair!" From that moment on, you are distracted from enjoying the true nectar of life.

To move forward as a family like the Rockefeller's, you must INTENTIONALLY relocate yourselves from a position of attachment to a position of detachment.

You must INTENTIONALLY bring yourselves from an entitlement-driven victim mentality to an outlook of caring and sharing.

You must INTENTIONALLY deliver yourselves from a mindset of resentment to a feeling of contentment.

And how can you do all that? By working with a trusted facilitator to develop a formal family governance protocol… and then sticking to the plan.

Chapter 13:

Cordero Family Update

*God has given us human beings the ultimate opportunity:
the ability to reflect on our lives, take charge of them,
and generate our own momentum.
What an amazing gift!*

I wish I could report that every one of the Cordero's problems has been resolved and that they are in perfect accord in every aspect of their lives, but of course that is not the case. That can never be true for any family because life is unpredictable and families are made up of imperfect human beings. There will always be challenges to overcome. For the Cordero's, the best we could hope for were baby steps because although they are brilliant when it comes to street smarts, they are not so skilled at holding a strategic vision for their family. They sometimes get hung up on nuances and fall back into the trenches.

The good news is that the family governance protocols and bylaws we established have provided them with direction, clarity and purpose so they can respond to the inevitable challenges in a healthier way. It took a solid two years for us to bring governance to this family, but it was two years well spent. We had to do some serious handholding, to the extent that we held multiple separate meetings with Diego and Maria and then Pedro and Julia, after which we had quarterly meetings for the entire family without any break. The purpose was to develop a system of checks and balances that Diego could accept as suitably rigorous without Pedro feeling too constrained. It has now reached a point where there is sufficient accountability. For the most part all family members are operating within the parameters that were set. Since they developed the protocols and policies together as a group, they own them... and that leads to greater compliance.

A healthy transition to the second generation leadership is well underway. Not only that, but the third generation is involved in perpetuating the family business: granddaughter Angelica has decided that she would like to take over the reins from her dad when the time comes. She recently enrolled in an MBA program and is spending as much time as she can in the office and in the field with Pedro.

As for Diego and Maria, things are improving for them at home, too. Now when something doesn't go the way Diego would like, he's more adept at handling it than he used to be. He's no longer boiling over with rage or pointing fingers and assigning blame to others. Instead he's working on ditching his victim mentality and becoming more detached so that he and Maria don't have to go through so much pain. He understands that detachment is liberation. He is learning to trust and let go, little by little. All of this has had a positive effect on Maria's health. She's relaxing for the first time in years and was recently able to stop taking antidepressants entirely.

Even though the Cordero's still have some rough edges that need to be smoothed out, they have made some wonderful gains in terms of family harmony. If you'll recall, one of the things that worried Diego and Maria most was that their grandchildren, Angelica and Andres, would lose track of their heritage. To reconnect them with their South American roots, we recommended that the entire family travel together to Diego and Maria's childhood village for a weeklong stay. The outcome of that trip was nothing short of miraculous. Diego and Maria were able to show their kids and grandkids their homeland for the first time. They explored the surrounding area, experiencing Mother Nature's glory together. They spent quality time with long lost family members and old friends, sharing meals, swapping stories, playing the music of their culture and dancing late into the night.

This experience had a profound effect on the second and third generations of the Cordero family. Whereas before the trip they had been grappling with the question of which type of philanthropy they wanted to engage in, after their return they had no doubt about what they wanted to do. The Cordero's are now working together to build a library and a medical clinic in their impoverished home village, thereby maintaining their connection with their roots and reinforcing family values while simultaneously making a difference in the world. This is values-based family philanthropy at its finest.

Not long ago we had the Cordero's fill out a new family harmony scorecard. **I'm happy to report that their score increased from their dismal benchmark of 22 percent to an impressive 75 percent.** They still have room for improvement, but they are committed to the journey.

It takes courage to step out of one's comfort zone; to turn away from one's old way of being. But the Cordero's have broken the mold. They are sharing and growing. They are perpetuating a legacy they can all be proud of.

PART 5:
AN INVITATION

Chapter 14:

Are You Ready to Share and Grow?

Regardless of your age or circumstances, you have within you the power to liberate yourself.

Whether your family is above-average like the Smith's or completely dysfunctional like the Cordero's and the Mehta's, you can shift everyone's mindset if you go about it the right way. As you've seen from the case studies in this book, age has nothing to do with it. It is all about mental readiness to change. When you're ready, you truly can transform every kinship relationship you have. Multi-generational harmony will not be just a wish. It will become a way of life. Discovery combined with sustainability, empathy combined with collaboration, and transparency combined with humility can create an amazing future for you and your family. When you liberate your self from all unwanted stuff, it create the abundance of space time and freedom to do what you want.

The examples I have used within this book have probably drawn a correlation to similar situations in your own life, and have given you better insights. However, it's not how much you know that counts but what you do with what you know. You now have a practical blueprint for the way forward. Don't let the simplicity of this blueprint fool you. Genius lies in simplicity, not complexity.

Superficiality or Sustainability: Your Choice.

Your self-proclaimed victory (being the youngest millionaire or billionaire, the wealthiest business leader in your community, the most respected physician in your specialty, whatever the case may be) is only short term. It is only superficial instant gratification. Can you sustain that for the next 25 years? Can you sustain that for the next 100 years? If you cannot, then it dies with you. The same is true of the sustainability of your values, legacy, vision and wisdom.

What is happening with the members of your family today? Are they grateful? Are they humble? Are they empathetic to the elders and those who were the founders through their sacrifice and commitment of time, talent and treasure for the growth of the business? Are all of you ready to stop complaining and moaning about what you don't have? If not, isn't that something you ought to address by way of an inner view of what really matters? Isn't it time for a paradigm shift, no matter what it takes?

I am reminded of John F. Kennedy's stirring message, "Ask not what your country can do for you. Ask what you can do for your country." Please take that statement and apply it to yourself as a benefactor, a stakeholder or a recipient of significant wealth and wisdom. Ask your conscience these questions: *What is my fiduciary role and my personal responsibility when it comes to the health and longevity of my family? What is one task I'm willing to undertake to make my forefathers extremely proud of how I have carried their values and wisdom into the new world?*

FAMILY LIFECYCLE STAGE AND ACTIONS

Dependent Apprenticeship (age 3-14)	• Responsibility : Develop Financial Vocabulary • Establish Early Financial Habits ant Values • Practice Saving, Spending, Earning and Philanthropy • Actions : MANAGE ALLOWANCE, HOLD FIRST JOB, BEGIN COMMUNITY INVOLVEMENT
Independent Starting Out (age 15-23)	• Test For communication style and values • Make Group Decision with Group Consequences • Actions : INVOLVE THEM IN FAMILY MEETING, TEST FOR COMMUNICATION STYLE, • TRY GROUP PHILOSOPHY
Interdependent Taking Charge (age 24-40)	• How do we add people to this Family • Build assets • Establist foundation for Family • Actions : ARE WE FARM TEAM FOR OTHER FAMILIES OR ARE WE ADDING TO OURS ? • ACQUIRE ASSETS, BUILD CAREER AND FAMILY, EXPLORE LIFE INTERESTS
Focus on Next Gen Influence this Gen (age 41-65)	• Take stock and Mentor G2 • Contribute to Next generation neeeds • ACTION : REASSESS LIFE CHOICES/GOALS AND ENERGIZE PLANS • WE ARE LIVING EXAMPLES TO NEXT GEN TO WATCH AND COPY;SET A GOOD EXAMPLE !EXAMPLE !
Succession Pass on the Torch (age 66+)	• Relinquish some responsibilities • Action : LIVE LIFE TO FULLEST • SHARE AND GROW

It doesn't matter whether your achievements are ever published to Facebook or LinkedIn or Instagram. Those are just toys that give you the space to present part of your experience (the part you're proud of!) to the world. The lifespan of those symptomatic things you are sharing with everyone on social media is less than one week, but the memories you have created and will create through your interactions with your grandparents, parents, siblings, children and grandchildren are ageless.

Wisdom is ageless.

Think about it… only one percent of the human race gets the privilege of experiencing great-grandparenthood. So if you are lucky, you'll get to witness four generations. Has anyone ever seen seven generations? Not that I know of. Wouldn't you like your footprint to stay alive for seven generations? There is a way you can do it, not because somebody is telling you to but because you WANT to. You may have to spend anywhere from one year to five years rebuilding the future for your family, but how bad would it be if at the end of five years, your family were to experience exponential growth? It would be time well spent, would it not?

Sustainability of your values can only happen if you are a fellow ascender, not a controlling leader. The fact that you created the wealth doesn't mean that you get to be demanding. You can't expect your family to blindly follow you on this journey of renewal just because you say so. They first have to accept you as a person they want to emulate and look up to. They have to see you as someone whose values they want to perpetuate, not by mandate but by choice. So you start your family on this path by walking it yourself first. To try and do otherwise will only lead to resentment, and you likely have plenty of that in your family already.

The way to kill resentment is through openness, humility, gratitude, sincerity and reciprocity.

Once you commit your heart and soul to this endeavor, your thought processes will change. When your thought processes change, your commitments, actions and behavior toward your loved ones will change. And when they witness the beautiful changes you've made, they will want to change too. Everything will change because you had the courage to take the first step toward shifting your family's collective mindset. It's either that or allow everyone to continue griping about your family's problems and faults.

That is your option.

And who's determining which path you will choose today? God? Absolutely not. God gives you thoughts but it's your attitude that makes the difference between capitalizing on the opportunity before you or maintaining the status quo. If you are stubborn and want to hold onto the mistaken notion that it's not you who needs to change but rather the others around you, then there is really no hope for your legacy.

Believe me when I tell you that the mind can perform miracles when it's properly channeled. For example, I know two people who have stayed alive for 45-years by ingesting nothing but honey and lemon water. No solid food whatsoever. This liquid diet has not adversely affected their efficiency. It has not affected their energy. It has not resulted in osteoporosis or hypertension. Nothing bad has come of it. They are completely healthy. They have such faith in what they're doing that their brain is literally working magic.

If these two people whom I know personally can exercise this kind of power over their lives—and there are hundreds of people like this right now in the world—don't you think you can liberate yourself from your victim mentality and entitlement mindset? Don't you think you can do some honest introspection with the goal of creating a family characterized by selfless sharing and continual growth? Because seriously, honest introspection is all it takes to begin liberating yourself.

Once you liberate yourself this way, your age will cease to matter. Your new journey, your mission and your purpose will allow you to live as long as you want. You will become a magnet that attracts people who don't have as much clarity, courage and commitment as you have demonstrated, and your example will show them the way. Humbly and without attachment to any preferred result, you will become more deeply engaged in life. You will become a calm, clear, unwavering communicator. Others will know that when you speak, it is gospel. They will move mountains to accommodate you and make the world the way you want it to be without you even having to ask. You will have zero expectation of receiving anything in return, yet you will accumulate miracle after miracle after miracle.

In short, you will be a shining example of how the best can get even better.

Imagine how that will affect the sustainability of your relationships, values and financial wealth? Sharing and growing becomes a path, a calling and a way of living rather than self-help. When you embrace it, your life will never be the same. You will never have regrets. You will see with your own eyes that the world is not as terrible and greedy as you have always been led to believe. This is not a hope, it is a reality.

And so I ask you now, are you ready to accept this blessing? If so, you must align yourself with someone who can show you the way, because as you learned from the families featured in this book, legacy perpetuation is not a do-it-yourself project.

Unconditional Surrender

When a person is in the midst of spiritual chaos, they may go to ten different divine masters trying to figure out who is the right one to bring them to peace. If their chaos is emotional, they may visit a dozen different therapists trying to find the one who offers a breakthrough. If their chaos is physical they may consult five different trainers before they connect with one who finally motivates them to make a change. They may read fifty different self-help books looking for inspiration, but all the books say the same thing: You take charge of your self and make it happen ! If you are not clear about your priorities, your purpose then your ability to transform your future will be affected.

This is the attitude that blocks you from going from chaos to comfort.

The way to come out of the chaos and achieve the comfort of clarity is to unconditionally surrender to a mentor who will empower you to facilitate change. This is a trusted person with whom you can become completely immersed because you understand that the journey they have traveled and the best practices they are living can positively impact you. They can help you find what matters and give you a deeper sense of your mission, vision and purpose in your life. If you don't capture those wonderful gifts that people in society are ready to share with you, then you will never sustain your legacy, your wealth and your wisdom beyond two generations.

Achieving clarity has everything to do with your mindset and the blessings you have in terms of finding a mentor or a mentor finding you. There is no shortcut.

I was fortunate enough to get priceless gifts of Clarity, vision, accountability, Empathy and Humility from several mentors and collaborators

Unless and until you have a mentor you can rely on unconditionally, your emotional, professional, financial, personal and physical growth cannot happen. Without growth in those aspects of your life, you become stagnant. You become docile. You become outdated. It's only a matter of time. The choice is strictly yours.

Obviously—for the sake of yourself and your family—I pray you will choose to move forward without delay. Reach out and take the hand that is extended to you now, and choose the path of Sharing and Growing. Your family's legacy of wealth and wisdom depends on it.

Chapter 15:

Values-based Family Governance

Amazing opportunities can't be properly seized by the complacent.
They are only fully seized by those who are humble...
and ready.

With all the dysfunction in the Cordero family, I knew it was going to be difficult for them to move from a place of attachment and discontent to a place of detachment, contentment, and unconditional acceptance of one another. But I also knew they could do it if they would trust the process and let go of their past commitments to being "right."

To begin, I explained to Diego, Maria, Pedro and Julia the five steps to healthy family governance.

5 Steps to Healthy Family Governance

Family Education
Giving benefactors an understanding of possible problems and solutions
Context: The Entrepreneur
VS
The Entrepreneur Family
Our Unique Story

Family Communication
Evaluation and Discussion in safe Family setting

Parents to make "The Call"

Healthy Family Governance
A DESTINATION
PUTTING IN ACTION
HORIZONTAL THINKING

Family Values and Meaningful Experiences

Stories of history and future mission vision and shared experience

Family Philanthropy

Test drive with parents and grandparent's money and shared values

The first is to recognize that family governance requires *horizontal thinking rather than vertical thinking.* Simply put, vertical thinking is about analysis; it's about using a formal step-by-step process to dig deep and find solutions. Vertical thinking emphasizes depth over breadth. Conversely, horizontal thinking emphasizes breadth over depth. It's about being visionary and applying outside-the-box creativity to finding solutions. To be successful at family governance, the Cordero's would need to get used to thinking horizontally. They'd need to open their minds and be prepared to cast a wide net when formulating their family's roadmap for the future.

The second step to healthy family governance is *family education.* It is critical that each benefactor achieve a thorough understanding of the real and potential problems facing the family as well as all the possible solutions. In doing so, the Cordero's would change the title and context of their story from "The Entrepreneur" to "The Entrepreneurial Family." The younger ones would also commit to learning as much as they could about entrepreneurship, investing, financial planning and tax planning. And they'd open their hearts and minds to being mentored by their elders.

The third step *is family communication.* Evaluations and discussions must occur in a safe and welcoming setting within a formal protocol, meaning that everyone has an opportunity to offer input without fear of rejection or ridicule. That said, the elders still have the final say if there is no consensus when a decision must be made.

Fourth is *sharing family values and meaningful experiences.* Getting the entire crew together with the sole intention of sharing a moment in time; this is where true magic can happen. This can consist of playing together, volunteering together, traveling together, eating together, worshipping together and engaging in educational opportunities together. Through these shared experiences, important information is exchanged.

The "Entrepreneurial Family" story is reinforced, helping the elders to pass on the family history and transfer their wisdom and values to the younger generations.

The final step to healthy family governance is family philanthropy. There is simply no better way to realign a family's focus and strengthen their cohesion than to get them working together on something they really care about; something that benefits other people. Toward that end, the entire Cordero family (including the grandkids, Angelica and Andres) would begin engaging in meaningful philanthropy based upon the values they share with their patriarch and matriarch.

Now that the Cordero's understood the steps, it was time to begin constructing their values-based family governance plan. Remember, creating such a plan is a process that unfolds over time. It is not something that can be done in one sitting. This was especially true for the Cordero's, who had an extremely difficult time letting go of their outmoded ways of interacting with one another.

As always, we reminded them to keep their focus on their strengths and not their weaknesses. The Cordero family's biggest strength was that they all had their hearts in the right place. All of them truly wanted their family to become stronger and more cohesive. This desire would become their saving grace. Whenever they encountered a challenge and seemed poised to slip back into their past dysfunctional behavior, we reminded them of the Cordero Family "ethos of life" as first expressed by their patriarch and matriarch:

- **Success is gained by hard work**

- **Be good to others**

- **Responsibility is always with me**

It took three years to create the Cordero's family governance plan, which was built around the answers to these questions:

- **How shall we make decisions?**

- **What will our code of conduct be?**

- **What will our leadership model be?**

- **How shall we accommodate the simultaneous goals of the family and the business?**

- **Who shall our advisors be? Who should be on our board of directors?**

- **How will we make this business grow? What should our strategy be?**

- **How will we communicate with non-family executives?**

- **What policies will we put in place?**

The deeper the Cordero's dove into answering these questions as a family, the more relaxed everyone became, especially Diego. Trying to singlehandedly steer his family's ship through stormy seas for decades had exhausted him. As we helped them work their way through the process, Diego gradually (very gradually!) began to step back and let Pedro take the wheel more and more.

Diego was especially pleased when we got down to answering the question about which policies should be in place for the business. Up to then there had been no official policies to guide Pedro in his decision making.

Consequently his judgments appeared to be haphazard and unsound, which led to much conflict between father and son.

To guide Pedro as he led the company forward (and to give Diego and Maria greater peace of mind), we developed formal policies for the following:

- **Conditions for ownership and voting rights**
- **Conflict resolution processes**
- **Dividend/Drawings**
- **Redemption process**
- **Business valuation methodology**
- **Buy-sell agreement (shareholder's agreement)**
- **Rights and responsibilities of non-employed owners**
- **Rules for travel and other major expenses**
- **Addressing family member's financial problems**

Next we developed processes for managing succession, managing differences, a constitution review and reporting. We also recommended structures for encompassing these processes, including a family council, a family business board, an independent board and a family office for investments. As you can imagine, all of this took a lot of hard work and focus on the part of the Cordero's. But the more they saw these elements finally falling into place, the more energized and inspired they became.

"I feel like the weight of the world is being lifted from my shoulders," Diego said during an early family meeting. "We haven't filled in all the blanks yet and we still have more than our share of disagreements, but at least we're moving forward as a family. At least we have a direction now."

ROAD MAP TO 10X LIFETIME GROWTH

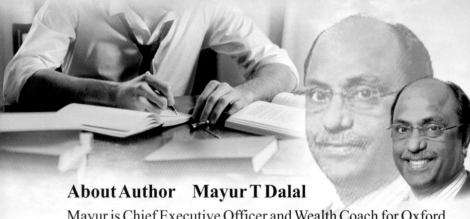

About Author   Mayur T Dalal

Mayur is Chief Executive Officer and Wealth Coach for Oxford Group of Lake Success Inc and Dalal Capital Advisors LLC. He has Degree in Chemical Technology and MBA from Elite Schools in Mumbai India.

He is Creator of The Legacy Perpetuator Process™ and Wealth Transfer with Wisdom™ . He has been helping 65 Multigenerational and Transnational Ultra High Net worth Families for last 29 years in developing 100 year Roadmap for Emotional and Financial Freedom. His focus on Helping Family businesses and Professionals create multigenerational bonding, and sustainable lifelong relationships along with preserving their wealth has made him most trusted professional and coach for most families he represent.

His ability to simplify complex issues and his clarity of vision to develop customized road map has helped several families achieve emotional freedom as well as tax efficient transfer of wealth.

Family Lifestyle Sustainability™, Family Venture Bank™ for Encouraging entrepreneurship and Family Heritage Bank™ to promote community Impact Initiatives has become cornerstone solutions for every family he has impacted.

His deep spiritual values combined with his passion has created integration of Heart and Head for every aspect of problem solving he does for Family's Estate, Charitable and Financial liquidity needs. He has become one of the most respected subject matter experts in the world for Cross Border Planning as well as Family Governance.

Blessings from Special people in my Life

"So often, extreme wealth becomes a destructive force in families. This book is filled with tools and stories of transformation to expand the thinking of and capability of any family caught in this all-too-common trap. Mayur Dalal's wisdom on the subject goes deep after years of passionate dedication to creating value for families who want to leave a powerful legacy and enrich their members in ways that go far beyond money."

Dan Sullivan
president, The Strategic Coach Inc

This book shares value of family harmony by relieving toxic energies and gaining empathy for families. Book has also shown inner core realization with understanding of antidotes to all toxic energies and raising the faith in family values with profound gratitude along with path of happiness.

Author is doctor of emotion, physical & financial health. his process gives emotional freedom.

We have achieved our emotional freedom with his help and highly recommend to read this valuable book to understand own family harmony and then get emotional freedom for happiness.

Ramesh Jhaveri
MD, FAAP, FACP.

In ancient Indian scripture it is said तेन त्यक्तेन भूजीथा*... sacrifice and you will achieve immense joy. One of the definition of family is, where everybody is prepare to sacrifice for each other.*

In this book Mayur Dalal, an expert in wealth management teaches us that if you want to be happy sacrifice for family. It is not wealth, but love and sacrifice are important to achieve true happiness.

I am sure by reading this book many people will achieve real peace and happiness in their family life.

Here you will find a powerful formula for happiness and mental peace.

Gulabbhai Jani
Founder
Sister Nivedita Educational Complex
Rajkot (India)

Acknowledgements

I express sincere gratitude to several people for their extraordinary contributions in writing this book.

I want to thank my parents for giving me gift of clarity of purpose and compassion to make difference in everyone's lives. My siblings for inspiring me and giving me gift of unconditional love. My wife Madhavi and Children Sagar and Reema for giving me gift of affection and selfless sacrifice.

I want to thank team at Oxford Group and Dalal capital Advisors for their excellent support. I want to thank Pamela Suarez for helping me writing this book. Dr.Rameshbhai Jhaveri, George Conniff, Dr Jatinbhai Shah, Drs Deena and Pravin Shah, Subodhbhai Amin, Ed Feiman, Bhavna and Mahesh Chhabria, Julie Schneider, Dr Jatinbhai Kapadia, Scott Fithian, Dan Sullivan and Chris Barber for their unwavering support in last 20 years to conceive the idea of capturing life experience in the form of book.

I also would like to acknowledge my closest friends Mukesh Khagram, Raman Jain and Mukesh Muchhala as my anchors in life.

There are exceptional contributions from Shri Kamleshbhai Sompura of Dotad for designing of book and cover, Shri Gulabbhai And Ushaben Jani of Sister Nivedita Trust for their years of insight and our Guru Brahm Swarup HDH Pramukh Swami Maharaj , Pragat Guru HDH Shri Mahant Swami Maharaj for empowering me with selfless attitude and make world better place. Finally I want to thank Girishbhai of Girish offset for printing.

Scorecard Title

Mindsets	1	2	3	4	5	6	7	8	9	10	11	12
1 Empathetic	I am apathetic to others issues			I have learnt during our life time to step up		I enjoy the experiences of being empath etic to all family family members		Being Empathetic is way of my life We put family first	
2 Listening Skills	I am strongly opinionated and argue a lot			I am getting better at listening to others view points		I have benefit ed a lot by acti vely liste ning to every one		I am excellent list ener	
3 Collaborative and Team driven	I am very self serving and mean to each other			I am becoming more aware abo ut benefit to collaborate		I have made progress and has improved in our collaborativ efforts		I genuinely care and colla borate with each other for everything	
4 Openness of communication	I am very secretive and close guarded			I am improving but long way to go		I have made progress in communicati ng with each others and open to discuss issues		I regularly communicate th e issues	
5 Aligned Values	I am very stubborn			I have become less stiff over last one year		I have made drastic changes in my att it ude and thus behavior		I compromise and let go to make every one else happy	
6 Accountability	I always blame others			I have begun taking my responsibility seriously		I have made t remendous progress in honoring all work assigned to me		Taking full accountabi lity is way of my life	
7 Trusting relationship	I am skeptical and cynical toward all			I am improving for last several years but have long way to go		i am cautious but lot more trusting		I trust every one in family	
8 Sharing	I donot like to share what I have			I am beginning to learn benefit of sharing		I have made lot of progress in sharing my experience and valuables with others		I have enjoyed sharing everything I have with all family members	

Your Determination and Endurance

Will Help You Achieve Emotional Freedeom